Hans Bayer reads the book of Ma[...] pher, the heart of a lover, and the [...] is to show how self-perception (b[...] individual and corporate) and God-perception shaped by the gospel simultaneously result in reconciled relationships and radical discipleship. Here is theology and biblical commentary at its best—rooted in powerful textual insights and rigorously applied to contemporary discipleship. The insights are profound; the grace is sweet.

—**Bryan Chapell,** President and Professor of Practical Theology, Covenant Theological Seminary, St. Louis

Oh, the limitations of an endorsement blurb! I could go on and on about Hans Bayer's new book, *A Theology of Mark*. Not only is this the best book I have ever read on the theology of Mark's Gospel, it's also my new favorite on the nature and rhythms of gospel-centered discipleship. My first response after finishing the book was to thank God for Hans's informed mind and enflamed heart—for this is exactly what Professor Bayer has given us as he interacts with the person and work of Jesus and our call to authentic discipleship. His reflection on Dietrich Bonhoeffer's *The Cost of Discipleship* is worth the price of the book alone. By all means, buy this book. It's not just a great read; it's an important read.

—**Scotty Smith,** Founding Pastor, Pastor of Preaching, Christ Community Church, Franklin, Tennessee

Hans Bayer gives us a remarkable study of the Gospel of Mark. No evangelical scholar is more aware of detailed and scholarly work on the Second Gospel than Dr. Bayer. In this volume, he displays his theological and pastoral insights into the Gospel. He deals with a number of major topics: genre, structure and purpose, thematic framework, and the person and work of Jesus. This brief work represents Dr. Bayer's decades of study and experience as a follower of Jesus. If you want to step into the theological and practical implications of the Gospel of Mark, this is the book for you. You will not be disappointed.

—**Richard L. Pratt Jr.,** President Third Millennium Ministries, Fern Park, Florida

A clear, careful, warm, detailed, reflective, humble, personal, and applicable consideration of Mark's presentation of Jesus and who we are in relation to him. Bayer's disarming gentleness enhances the pointedness of Mark's claims about Jesus and about my need to surrender to the Carpenter from Galilee. This is an encouragement toward taking up our crosses as Jesus' people, particularly amid the challenges of twenty-first-century North America and Europe. Use the book in a small group and see what happens.

—**J. Nelson Jennings,** Director of Program and Community Life, Overseas Ministries Study Center, New Haven

There is a great hunger for Christ-centered discipleship. And what better place to be instructed in such grace-centered living than at the feet of Jesus himself? *A Theology of Mark* deserves to be studied both as to its theory and even more importantly as to its practice. May it be used by many to strengthen their relationship with Christ and lead them in true biblical discipleship.

—**Paul D. Kooistra,** Coordinator of Mission to the World, Presbyterian Church in America (PCA), Atlanta

Hans Bayer's character-shaping tour through Mark's Gospel will bring each reader who longs for intimacy with a holy God to an intensely intimate and more dependent encounter with Jesus. In his insightful and compelling book, Bayer has found a way to help us listen clearly to the very words and actions of the Savior that call us into relationship with himself and lead toward magnified kingdom impact. Discipleship leaps forward not simply as a duty, but as a passionate desire of God to be near to us.

—**Benjamin K. Homan,** President, John Stott Ministries / Langham Partnership (USA)

Having already benefited enormously from his teaching on the subject and seen it deeply impact young Christian leaders in Scotland, I am thrilled to see Hans Bayer's material in print and available to a wider audience. I am confident that it will become a key resource for us in shaping our theology and practice of discipleship.

Paying close attention to the wider literary structures as well as the textual details of Mark's Gospel, Hans calls us back to a biblically and theologically rigorous understanding of discipleship patterned on Jesus' example and teaching. This book is unique in framing Jesus' call to discipleship in the context of the bigger biblical picture of redemptive history. The emphases on radical dependence, heart transformation, and the reciprocal nature of disciple-making relationships provide necessary correctives to contemporary approaches that are too often marred by individualism, a focus on activities to the neglect of the heart, and a misuse of power by leaders who are "discipling" others.

This material on discipleship in the Gospel of Mark represents the fruit of many years of deep engagement with the text as well as mature reflection on its application to the reality of living as a disciple of Jesus. Hans is a wise and godly instructor whose life matches his teaching. This book is a deep and rich repository of insight and wisdom that needs to be engaged, wrestled with, and applied by those called to lead within the body of Christ. I am convinced that as we apply the principles Hans Bayer so brilliantly draws out from Mark, we will see not only the transformation of individual disciples, but also the transformation of church and society. Hans points us back to Jesus' approach to discipleship—why would we ever seek another?

—**Mark Stirling,** Leader of the European Disciple-Making Leaders Network, Edinburgh

In customary fashion, Dr. Hans Bayer provides high-level scholarship in accessible form in his latest work. For those looking for a fresh way to love Jesus with the mind and the heart, this book provides that rich possibility. I highly recommend it.

—**Scott Sauls,** Senior Director of Community Formation, Redeemer Presbyterian Church, New York

A Theology of Mark

Dad,

   I thought you might appreciate
the insights of one of my favorite
professors (a good, full-blooded German)
as you continue to mine the depths
of Mark's gospel.

love,

Jenilyn

Christmas 2012

Explorations in Biblical Theology

Anointed with the Spirit and Power:
The Holy Spirit's Empowering Presence

The Elder: Today's Ministry Rooted in All of Scripture

Election and Free Will: God's Gracious Choice
and Our Responsibility

Life Everlasting: The Unfolding Story of Heaven

The Nearness of God: His Presence with His People

Our Secure Salvation: Preservation and Apostasy

A Theology of James: Wisdom for God's People

A Theology of Mark: The Dynamic between
Christology and Authentic Discipleship

Wisdom Christology: How Jesus Becomes God's Wisdom for Us

Robert A. Peterson, series editor

A Theology of Mark

The Dynamic between Christology and Authentic Discipleship

Hans F. Bayer

P U B L I S H I N G
P.O. BOX 817 • PHILLIPSBURG • NEW JERSEY 08865-0817

Library of Congress Cataloging-in-Publication Data

Bayer, Hans F. (Hans Friedrich)
 A theology of Mark : the dynamic between Christology and authentic discipleship / Hans F. Bayer.
    p. cm. -- (Explorations in biblical theology)
 Includes bibliographical references and indexes.
 ISBN 978-1-59638-119-3 (pbk.)
 1. Bible. N.T. Mark--Theology. I. Title.
 BS2585.52.B39 2012
 226.3'06--dc23
                                2011047703

To my wife, Susan,
faithful friend and sojourner in following Christ

Contents

CONTENTS

Series Introduction

BELIEVERS TODAY need high-quality literature that attracts them to good theology and builds them up in their faith. Currently, readers may find several sets of lengthy—and rather technical—books on Reformed theology, as well as some that are helpful and semipopular. Explorations in Biblical Theology takes a more mid-range approach, seeking to offer readers the substantial content of the more lengthy books, while striving for the readability of the semipopular books.

This series includes two types of books: (1) some treating biblical themes and (2) others treating the theology of specific biblical books. The volumes dealing with biblical themes seek to cover the whole range of Christian theology, from the doctrine of God to last things. Representative early offerings in the series focus on the empowering by the Holy Spirit, justification, the presence of God, preservation and apostasy, and substitutionary atonement. Examples of works dealing with the theology of specific biblical books include volumes on the theology of 1 and 2 Samuel, the Psalms, and Isaiah in the Old Testament, and books on the theology of Mark, Romans, and James in the New Testament.

Explorations in Biblical Theology is written for college seniors, seminarians, pastors, and thoughtful lay readers. These volumes are intended to be accessible and not obscured by excessive references to Hebrew, Greek, or theological jargon.

Each book seeks to be solidly Reformed in orientation, because the writers love the Reformed faith. The various theological themes and biblical books are treated from the perspective of biblical theology. Writers either trace doctrines through the Bible or open up the theology of the specific book they treat.

ix

Writers desire not merely to dispense the Bible's good information, but also to apply that information to real needs today.

Explorations in Biblical Theology is committed to being warm and winsome, with a focus on applying God's truth to life. Authors aim to treat those with whom they disagree as they themselves would want to be treated. The motives for the rejection of error are not to fight, hurt, or wound, but to protect, help, and heal. The authors of this series will be godly, capable scholars with a commitment to Reformed theology and a burden to minister that theology clearly to God's people.

Robert A. Peterson
Series Editor

Acknowledgments

TO THANK SOME, but not all, of those who have been influential in the inception and maturing of the present book is a sure recipe for hurting some good friends who perhaps contributed most significantly to it. I thus wish to thank my adult children; relatives; friends; colleagues (especially "my educator," Donald Guthrie); and UCCF/Navigator conference participants in Arbroath, Scotland; as well as my students in St. Louis, Riga, Kiev, Eger, and Goiania as a group to whom I am deeply indebted for friendship and counsel. A special mention is due to those wonderful IFES "Bible and Culture" participants at Schloss Mittersill, Austria, who came from Western, Central, and Eastern Europe, as well as all the way from Asia. All of you have shaped me and my thinking more than you can imagine. God has richly blessed me through each one of you. Thank you.

Without the generous sabbatical arrangement at Covenant Theological Seminary and the support of our wonderful staff (including our library staff), administration, colleagues, and the board of trustees, I would not have had time to write. The sabbatical afforded my wife and me use of the library and research facility at Schloss Mittersill, Austria, to accomplish much of the work on this project.

My colleague, Robert Peterson, kindly invited me to contribute this book to the series he so ably edits, Explorations in Biblical Theology. He supported and encouraged me in countless ways throughout the process. My teaching assistant, Elliott Pinegar, helped me with many references, and Rick Matt edited the entire book in a most competent and helpful fashion. Thank you. Marvin

Padgett and the other team members at P&R Publishing kindly supported the project in its various stages.

My wife, Susan, has been a constant friend and companion along the adventurous road. It is a joy to dedicate this book to her. In the course of writing it and teaching some of its contents, we discovered even more common ground for the kind of team ministry that delights us both.

Introduction

SINCERE CHRISTIANS hold helpful yet divergent ideas about discipleship. Some focus on steps that disciples must follow, some emphasize one-on-one mentoring based on the relationship of Paul and Timothy, others see the practice of spiritual disciplines as the key, while still others hold to an intellectual approach that accentuates reading and studying good books.

While all of these approaches have something to recommend them, they also share common weaknesses. They do not appear to draw their definitions of discipleship from Scripture's big picture. And although their proponents look to Jesus for salvation, they do not focus enough on his view of discipleship.

This book is an attempt to remedy this situation. Though there is value in other approaches to discipleship, our purpose here is to explore a more comprehensive approach—that of Jesus with his own disciples. Though we will be concerned with details, we will also attempt to put those details in the context of the biblical story and worldview. Consequently, many readers will be surprised—perhaps as surprised as the original band of disciples.

The twelve initial companions of Jesus, chief among them Peter, were indeed taken by surprise, as John Mark's presentation of Peter's account reveals. The account is honest, self-critical, transparent, and unadorned. The group with which Jesus works admits to disbelief and the inability to comprehend key aspects of his person and teaching. The Master is portrayed as incomprehensible and yet deeply personal, puzzling yet captivating, awesome yet the harbor of profound hope. What has been revealed about the purposes of God in the Old Testament is brought by the disciples' Master to a perplexing yet exhilarating realization. In the wake of this realization, preconceived expectations held among Jews in first-century Palestine are shattered to make room for the unexpected yet deeply biblical appearance of "him who is to come." The question "Who is he?" (Mark 4:41; 8:28) reverberates throughout Mark's (and thus Peter's) account as a leading theme. Connected with this question is Jesus' challenging exposure of the disciples' true need. In the end, the profound claims laid upon Mark's readers are a consequence of the eminent stature, sacrificial commitment, and transforming power of the Master, as well as his knowledge of the human heart.

As we turn our attention from this first-century A.D. witness account to our own time, we are at once struck by the fact that we live in a fast-moving age, especially in the Western world. Modernism (ca. 1790–1960) with its man-centered rationalism has been replaced by postmodernism (ca. 1960–2010?) with its man-centered experience and self-realization. Some have already coined the term "transmodernism" to describe the philosophical and experiential milieu we are now entering.

Even if these labels are not helpful, the void left by the profound tragedies of twentieth-century fascism and communism and the recent resurgence of radical Islam have led to great disillusionment, cynicism, and animosity. In the midst of a moral and spiritual void, especially in Europe, many call for a return to a form of rationalism[1] as the only way out of the current impasse and the perceived threat of radical Islam.

Yet one common sentiment does seem to be pervasive: Christianity has been tested intellectually and practically over the past twenty centuries and has been found wanting, at least in the Western world (think of the "New Atheism"). Often, however, it is a mere caricature of Christianity that is being rejected, a caricature which misrepresents the truth and essence of the faith. This caricature is propagated by well-meaning and not so well-meaning people claiming to represent the faith of Christians while actually peddling their own misguided, misleading, and, at

---

1. We see a call for a return to a modified Kantian rationalism and ethics in, for example, Jürgen Habermas.

times, very harmful brand of "Christianity" (such as, for example, the "health-and-wealth" message).

At a time of great confusion and profound need, a fresh look at the person of Jesus, the purpose of his life on earth, and his relevance for the twenty-first century is sorely needed. To this end, we will focus on the Gospel of Mark as an early and reliable witness-report of the astounding person and transforming mission of Jesus in the context of the in-breaking, eternal rule of God.

We will relate the ancient witness account to today's world. Before we make this connection, however, we will briefly seek to answer the following questions:

1. What is the genre of this ancient witness account (chapter 1), and how was the content of that account collected (in chapter 1 and appendix A)?
2. What formal structure, purpose, and flow of thought does the account display (chapter 2)?
3. What thematic framework serves as the backdrop for the call to follow Christ (chapter 3)?
4. Who is this Jesus in his person, mission, and power (chapter 4)?

Appendix A will take up contemporary challenges concerning the origin and formation of Mark's Gospel account, and offer some responses to those challenges.

To proceed in this way, we neither abandon long-standing questions of historical and theological truth nor ignore pressing contemporary questions of authenticity, relevance, and significance for everyday life. We submit that both "truth questions" (chapter 1 and appendix A) and "relevance questions" (chapters 2–9) are appropriate and necessary. The Markan Gospel account has to be able to withstand scrutiny on both counts and give answers to both areas of investigation.

A fashionable and substantial wing of modern scholarship still argues that the canonical Gospel of Mark is a faith-driven construction of the early church; such arguments must be answered (see chapter 1 and appendix A). Likewise, it is not sufficient and satisfactory to argue simply that the message of Mark is life-changing and relevant (chapters 2–9) regardless of whether it is historically true or not. If Mark is merely a creative faith-projection of the early church, its life-changing message is unsubstantiated and ultimately meaningless.

Nor will it do to readily accept the Gospel of Mark as historically true (see chapter 1 and appendix A) while being unable to awaken a modern person from a materialistic slumber or existential cynicism. Such a challenge can only be answered with the evidence of individual and communal lives lived in the transforming power of the gospel of God's grace. Only changed lives will show the contemporary viability of Jesus' unusual and counterintuitive call to surrender self-sufficiency in exchange for following him—and thus, God (chapters 4–9).

In our central section (chapters 4–8) we will argue that at the beginning of Jesus' unique and authoritative call to discipleship lie two essential questions (chapter 5):

1. Who do you perceive yourself to be?
2. Who do you perceive God to be?

Even atheists, agnostics, and materialists must offer answers to both questions by stating, for example, the belief that God does not exist or that God is unknowable. The consequence of such statements is that such a person exists for him- or herself and that there is no absolute foundation for distinguishing good and evil. The two questions apply especially to our contemporaries who hold to some belief in a higher being or existence.

The baffling realization is that both questions are intimately interconnected: human identity and life story are either conceived of as autonomous or in relationship to a loving Creator. If they are autonomous, one is challenged to come up with definitions arising out of him- or herself, that is, for instance, by recourse to naturalistic evolution, assuming the existence of a random universe without cause.[2]

If, however, identity and life story are conceived of as being in dependence upon a loving Creator, relationship with him has to be addressed in the context of human existence. In this context, new questions arise: is the relationship between God and man seriously broken (Christianity), or is it more or less intact, capable of being improved by mere spiritual disciplines and knowledge (rabbinic Judaism, Islam, and, to a degree, Confucianism, Hinduism, and Buddhism)? The interdependence of the two questions is undeniable for the atheist, agnostic, and the theist.

Jesus' initial and authoritative call to discipleship addresses this interconnected pair of questions in a confounding and challenging way. He claims that his disciples do not know the answer to either core question and are thus incapable of participating meaningfully in the purpose of individual and corporate existence as designed by the Creator.

Mark's testimony to Jesus claims nothing less than the following: the eternal Son of God entered this world by incarnation in order to resolve this baffling pair of core problems facing human beings, both individually and corporately. Initially, Jesus calls for a radical assessment of self-perception and God-perception in order to lead to a reconciled relationship with the true God, self, and others. This reconciled relationship with God is the essential foundation for transformed identity, character, and life.

The identity-shaping answer to these two core questions molds our character, attitudes, decisions, and actions (chapters 6 and 7) toward God, ourselves, and others. Particular expressions of discipleship thus arise from a fundamentally renewed relationship with the triune God and a true, God-centered view of ourselves and others. The disciplines of discipleship are never to be pursued in autonomy or self-sufficiency. Rather, they grow out

2. So Richard Dawkins, *The God Delusion* (New York: Houghton Mifflin Harcourt, 2006), in contrast to John Lennox, *God's Undertaker: Has Science Buried God?* (Oxford, UK: Lion-Hudson, 2009), and James Le Fanu, *Why Us? How Science Rediscovered the Mystery of Ourselves* (New York: Harper Press, 2009).

of a reconciled relationship with God and a personal realization of the need to be radically transformed. Thus confronted, we come to understand deeply that we are broken persons in need of both individual and communal transformation, healing, and purification.

Spiritual fruit such as ongoing surrender to God, faith, prayer, watching over our hearts, humility, forgiveness, steadfastness in the midst of persecution, and courageous proclamation of the gospel arise from a sober self-assessment of both brokenness and fragile beauty progressively renewed in relationship with the loving God. This holds true for any spiritual exercise or act.

The final outcome of Christ's call to discipleship is God-dependent, Christlike individuals and communities maturing in the context of the unending rule of God. And these maturing, transformed people and communities are called to have a transformative influence on their personal, cultural, economic, scientific, and political surroundings until Christ returns (see chapter 9). Authentic witness to Jesus brings forth authentic discipleship in the context of the growing messianic kingdom of God.

Part 1

Mark as Biography and Message of God's Eternal Rule

Mark as Biography and Memorized Witness Account

Mark's Use of the Ancient Genre of Bios

In antiquity, the general maxim held true that "form serves content." This means that formal analyses guide the reader in the proper understanding of content. Determining the genre of Mark's account thus serves to identify how the hearer or reader is meant to interpret the content. Should the text be taken as a fictitious story, a philosophical treatise, an historical novel, or a biographical sketch? This determination guides the audience in its author-intended expectation, since the author conveys objective hints by means of his selection of genre.

Mark identifies his account in 1:1 as "good news" (gospel). In the following discussion, we must briefly clarify what Mark's explicit description "good news" signifies and what the literary character (genre) of this "gospel" is.

Simply put, Mark's Gospel is an account of "good news"[1] containing both descriptions of events and messages. As the Markan Gospel account is analyzed in terms of its specific characteristics,[2] it fits best the general genre of ancient bios. In other words: Mark claims to present a biographical sketch (*bios*) of a hero, containing descriptions of events and messages as good news.

---

1. In the Greco-Roman world the term conveys an imperial proclamation, e.g., of a military victory.
2. Genre can be defined in simple terms as a recurring, recognizable literary pattern.

Typically, the ancient format of bios includes a brief introduction (with an optional infancy section), then proceeds to give
select anecdotes (stories, dialogues, special events, characteristic
statements) depicted from the mature years of the main character, and ends with a description of how the main character died,
often asking whether or not he denied what he stood for during
his lifetime. What is unique in the type of bios Mark presents is
the fact that the (innocent) death of the main character is not
only mentioned but featured as the character's life goal. The fact
that the hero dies by shameful crucifixion is a problem only if
his innocence is uncertain.

It would be wrong to compare such an ancient bios-account
with the literary form of a modern comprehensive biography.
What this ancient genre indicates is that Mark functions within
Greco-Roman and Jewish conventions of his time which intend
to give reliable biographical data while not giving an exhaustive
life story.

Unlike historical-critical scholarship, which often denies
that much of Mark's account is historically authentic, the term
"good news" and the genre of Mark's Gospel account both claim
historical authenticity and an authoritative message. The good
news, cast in the genre of bios as ancient biography, suggests that
Mark intends to convey both a credible historical witness account
and an appeal (in fact, Christ's appeal), drawing attention to the
significance of the recounted events. The gospel genre of bios,
conveying good news, portrays itself as proclamation through
historical witness.[3]

In an extensive study, Richard Burridge[4] analyzes ten differently dated Greco-Roman biographies and concludes that
the Gospels conform to the (rather flexible) literary genre of

---

3. See Martin Hengel, *Crucifixion in the Ancient World and the Folly of the Message
of the Cross* (Minneapolis: Augsburg Fortress, 1977).

4. Richard A. Burridge, *What Are the Gospels? A Comparison with Graeco-Roman
Biography* (Cambridge: Cambridge Univ. Press, 1992). A summarizing essay, "About
People, by People, for People: Gospel Genre and Audiences," by Burridge appeared in
Richard Bauckham, ed., *The Gospels* (Grand Rapids: Eerdmans, 1997), 113–45. See also
Paul Barnett, *Jesus and the Rise of Early Christianity. A History of New Testament Times*
(Downers Grove, IL: InterVarsity, 1999), 137.

(religious) *bioi* rather than to alternate genres such as "philosophical treatises," "deeds of heroes," "memoirs of heroes," the genre of the "Jewish apocalyptic drama," or accounts of "divine men."[5] Accounts of "divine men," for example, narrate their subject's miracles, martyrdoms, and metamorphoses into divine beings, thus displaying significant differences from the approach of the canonical Gospels. Among them are: (1) the genre of these accounts is difficult to determine; (2) many of these collections postdate the canonical Gospels; and (3) parallels to the canonical Gospels are limited to superficial analogies.[6] While Jesus also performs miracles, his kingdom-mission provides a context and purpose for his miracles. This aspect is conspicuously missing in the accounts of "divine men."

Bioi in antiquity primarily describe the mature life of key persons who are mentioned at the beginning of the accounts. A simple chronological sequence, especially noticeable at the beginning and end of an account, is complemented by various thematic insertions in the middle section. *Bioi* rely on oral and written sources concerning the hero's actions and words to provide an anecdotal biographical sketch of the hero. These biographical descriptions are mostly serious in tone and display respect for the hero.

Paul Barnett[7] further differentiates Burridge's conclusions by stating that the canonical passion accounts run, to a degree, counter to the general bios genre. While classical bios-accounts observe the way in which an important figure dies,[8] including the dying person's last words, nowhere besides the canonical Gospels is there the notion that the goal of the main character's life was to die. Nor is there an explicit acknowledgment elsewhere of the most shameful and offensive

5. See Burridge, "About People," in: Richard Bauckham, *The Gospels*, 113–45.
6. See W. R. Telford, *Mark* (Sheffield: Sheffield Academic Press, 1996), 97, and especially Barry Blackburn, *Theios Aner* (Philadelphia: Coronet Books, 1990), 13–72.
7. Paul Barnett, *Jesus and the Rise of Early Christianity* (Downers Grove, IL: InterVarsity, 1999), 159.
8. Burridge, *What Are the Gospels?*, 142–49.

form of execution by crucifixion. And finally, there is no parallel in other bios-accounts to the liberating and reconciling effect of the hero's death. Barnett's observations also support the notion that the Gospel account as bios is both historical witness and proclamation.

A final important observation regarding bios is that the character of its hero is often intended to be imitated by the reader/ hearer.[9] This raises the intriguing question as to what degree the very genre of Mark's account hints that Jesus' person and actions are to be imitated by his followers. We will argue that Jesus teaches, exemplifies, and above all enables "pattern-imitation" among his followers rather than simply calling for a simplistic, self-generated "copying of Christ." But we must take note of a "pattern-imitation theme" embedded in the genre itself.

Mark as a Systematically Memorized Witness Account

Mark's account of the "good-news-about-(and from)-Jesus" seems to fit well into the ancient genre of bios. Mark was thus written with the intent of providing a reliable sketch of Jesus' public appearances with the additional aim of engendering a form of pattern-imitation. As we will see, the kind of imitation contained in the message of this bios-account is solidly based on Jesus' own teaching and work as he enables his followers to grow in core values, attitudes, and actions.

Under Jesus' tutelage, the first disciples underwent a systematic memorization and training period in order to retain core elements of his teaching and actions. He also gave them a grid of interpretation for understanding his significance and that of his mission.

Jesus was an intentional teacher. The contents of his "curriculum" focused on a true understanding of both God's messianic rule and the identity and function of God's Messiah. The

9. David B. Capes, "Imitatio Christi and the Gospel Genre," *Bulletin for Biblical Research* 13.1 (2003): 1–19.

disciples, who had already been trained biblically in their own homes and especially in synagogue schools (from about age 7 to age 14), learn from Jesus in the same way they learned in their synagogue schools—by memorization. In each case, memorization preceded understanding.

However, Jesus' teaching style exceeds that of the synagogue teachers by:

1. his contextualizing the learning process in real-life settings and dialogues, life-on-life teaching, and mentoring;
2. his authority further accentuating his teaching and embedding truths in the disciples' minds and hearts long before they truly understand;
3. his complementing this memorization process through the agency of the Holy Spirit (John 14:15–31; 16:4–24), who assists the disciples in recalling what Jesus had previously taught them.

Following is a brief overview of some of the elements that scholars[10] have presented to illuminate the elementary educational pattern in first-century Palestine. They argue that this furnishes the most convincing background for "Jesus as teacher" and thus for schematic and stereotyped oral transmission of the gospel witness prior to its written fixation. Jesus used among his initial disciples pedagogical principles similar to those used in elementary school education, in synagogue services, and in Jewish homes.[11] He did so in order to embed a memorized body of information in his disciples. The Gospel of Mark was then composed from a relatively wide pool of systematically memorized material.

10. Cf., e.g., Rainer Riesner, *Jesus als Lehrer: Eine Untersuchung zum Ursprung der Evangelien-Überlieferung*, 3rd ed. (Tübingen: Mohr Siebeck, 1988) ; Birger Gerhardsson, *Memory and Manuscript* (Lund: CWK Gleerup, 1964 [Eng. trans.]); idem., *Tradition and Transmission in Early Christianity* (Lund: Gleerup, 1964); idem., *The Origins of the Gospel Tradition* (Philadelphia: Fortress, 1979); Henry Wansbrough, ed., *Jesus and the Oral Gospel Tradition* (Sheffield: JSOT, 1991).

11. See Riesner, *Jesus als Lehrer*, 151–206, 137–51, and 102–18, respectively.

Elementary School Education in First-Century Palestine[12]

Elementary school education in first-century Palestine focused on oral transmission and retention of mainly written tradition (especially the Hebrew Old Testament).

The Schoolhouse. By the time Jesus taught in Palestine, Pharisees (and their predecessors) had long-established schools for the purpose of teaching the Torah to young boys. In Tiberias alone, some thirteen schools existed. The general pattern in first-century Judaism was to operate an elementary school in each of the widely spread synagogues, as well as, at times, an advanced school for students of the Torah and oral traditions.

The Teacher. Besides the task of teaching, the elementary school teacher was, at times, expected to serve as the synagogue attendant as well as a scribe (a copyist of manuscripts). Usually these elementary teachers received some recompense for their work, while the advanced teachers of the law had begun the habit of refraining from accepting pay several decades prior to Christ. In the eyes of advanced Torah teachers, elementary school teachers were thus inferior. This may have contributed to the trend in Jewish society to view elementary school teachers as part of the lower class of society.

The Student. Most boys in Jewish Palestine began their formal education at age seven and ended it by age fourteen.[13] School was held every day from sunup to sundown, except on the Sabbath. In the afternoon of each Sabbath, however, fathers would examine their sons on material learned during the previous week.

Contents to Be Learned. Learning various sections of the Hebrew Bible by heart lay at the center of elementary school edu-

12. For this and the following description of synagogue elementary education, see Riesner, *Jesus als Lehrer.*
13. See, e.g., Josephus, *Life,* 7–9, who apparently completed elementary education at age fourteen.

cation. Of great importance was the memorization of liturgically important sections of Scripture (such as the "Shema" in Deuteronomy 6:4 and the Hallel Psalms 114–18), as this became useful for both the life of an adult Jew and his future participation in synagogue services.[14] At times, even Greek was taught in these schools. Tiberias and Sepphoris (a few miles north of Nazareth), for instance, had Greek-speaking members in their respective synagogues.

Methods of Instruction. Learning by heart[15] constituted the focus of education. Therefore, rote memorization was much more emphasized than creative, independent combination of facts or independent thinking. Proverbs 1–9, for instance, had to be memorized mechanically long before the message these chapters convey was understood and applied. The key to success was repetition.[16] Tradition holds that Hillel once remarked: "He who repeats his passage one hundred times is not to be compared with him who repeats his passage a hundred and one times."[17] Various mnemonic aids were employed to reach the stated goal. A good number of biblical texts already contained such aids, such as alliteration (cf. Prov. 18:20–22) and acrostic poetry (cf. Prov. 31:10–31; Ps. 119). Further aids were metric structure as well as the use of paronomasia (wordplay) and cantillation (murmur). Additional mnemonic devices, such as "question and answer" or having the teacher begin a verse and letting the student finish, were common. All this was carried out with strict discipline.

Similarities and Dissimilarities with Jesus' Approach to Teaching

Similarities. There are striking methodological parallels between elementary school education in the first century A.D. and Jesus' pedagogical approach. This suggests that he intentionally

14. Furthermore, learning the skills of reading and writing (by copying and dictation) was likewise accomplished by the use of Scriptures. Learning how to read often began with Leviticus, since it contained difficult texts. This was to prevent the pupils from guessing.

15. See also the oral traditions in Egypt, Mesopotamia, Greece, and Rome.

16. Cf. Josephus, *Against Apion*, 2.178.

17. Riesner, *Jesus als Lehrer*, 194.

15

utilized these familiar methods of instruction. On account of this correspondence, the historical reconstruction of how the Gospels came into existence may be explainable in terms of the Gospel writers making use of fixed, stereotyped oral (and partially written) learning. Riesner points especially to the following facts:

- Jesus employs these methods of instruction in order to assure faithful transmission. The stereotyped method is visible in Jesus' references to and interpretations of Scripture, his use of summaries, and the rich employment of various Jewish figures of speech (*mašal*). Jesus' teaching style includes brevity, imagery, and the use of vivid language. He uses parallelism, rhythm, rhyme, chiasm, pairs, alliteration, assonance, and aphorisms. He also connects events with instruction and involves himself in memorable dialogues and controversial discussions.
- The disciples provide the personal continuity of tradition between Jesus' life and teaching and the beginnings of the messianic church. We note in this context the movement from "disciple" to "apostle," or "sent one."[18] The intent of all this is to facilitate memorization and preserving the continuity of witness-tradition.

Dissimilarities.[19] The following additional elements employed by Jesus are not typical for elementary school education, yet they accentuate Jesus' intent to embed stereotyped memory in his initial followers.

- The community which Jesus develops with his disciples surpasses that of the (sometimes close) pupil-teacher relationships. This intensifies the learning process.

18. See Herman Ridderbos, *Redemptive History and the New Testament Canon of Scripture* (Phillipsburg, NJ: Presbyterian and Reformed, 1988), concerning the kerygmatic, apostolic, and teaching ministry of the disciples of Christ, all elements of which point back to the Christ of history.
19. For the following, see Riesner, *Jesus als Lehrer*, 297–496.

- Jesus calls his pupils prophetically;[20] they do not simply come to him as was the case in advanced Torah schools (e.g., Saul of Tarsus seeking to be trained under Gamaliel). This factor emphasizes the initiative of the teacher to form and shape the pupil.[21]
- Parallel to this, Jesus' unusual authority (including his "I am" and "Amen" sayings) is without analogy in Judaism.
- The fact that Jesus sends out his disciples in pairs to teach and practice his instruction deepens learning and relationships while the message is being spread.
- A further factor in stereotyped memorization is the fact that the disciples report to Jesus what they had taught, accomplished, and failed in (Mark 6:30).
- Jesus teaches as an itinerant teacher and prophet, thus exposing the disciples to extensive repetition with slight variations. John Wenham notes: "It is inevitable that an itinerant preacher must repeat himself again and again, sometimes in identical words, sometimes with slight variations, sometimes with new applications; sometimes an old idea will appear in an entirely new dress."[22] Part of the literary symmetry and variation of the Gospels may thus be traceable to verbatim or near-verbatim repetitions and variations by Jesus himself.

The above-mentioned circumstances of stereotyped oral transmission are fundamental for reliable transmission of Jesus' teaching. Conservative collection and systematic transmission through oral and written means thus mark the general attitude toward his teaching (see Acts 20:35; 1 Cor. 7:10; 1 Cor. 11:23–25).[23]

---

20. Cf. Barnett, *Jesus and the Rise of Early Christianity*, 140.
21. Ibid.
22. John W. Wenham, "Synoptic Independence and the Origin of Luke's Travel Narrative," *New Testament Studies* 27 (1981): 507–15 [509].
23. Cf. Earle Ellis, "Preformed Traditions and Their Implications for Pauline Christology," in *Christology, Controversy and Community*, ed. David Horrell and Christopher Mark Tuckett (Leiden: Brill, 2000), 303–20, esp. 310.

It must also be noted that there is considerable evidence that at least some of the disciples were bilingual, speaking Aramaic and Greek. This provides the assurance that Jesus' "curriculum" was safely transmitted from Aramaic to Greek. In appendix A, we provide a brief description of how the Gospel of Mark was most likely composed from such stereotyped oral learning of the disciples and cast in the genre of ancient bios.

Conclusion

We can summarize by stating that John Mark, by way of Peter,[24] receives selections from a stereotyped and systematically memorized body of material containing "good news" about and from Jesus. The selections are cast in the genre of an ancient biographical account (bios), all of which is to shape and influence the readers/hearers in a significant way. Their lives are to be profoundly transformed by what they hear and read in Mark's Gospel.

24. See appendix A.

2

Mark's Structure, Purpose, and Flow of Thought

THE DISCUSSION OF narrative structure, outline, plot, purpose, and flow of thought contributes to the understanding of Mark's message ("form serves content"), and serves to identify in more detail the central points and concepts the author wishes to communicate.

We have already noted that genre analysis helps determine the point of reference and what readers expect; genre communicates to the reader the overall framework of what the writer intends to communicate (a novel, a drama, an essay; in our case, an historical document). Analysis of genre thus conveys to the reader what claims the author intends to make (e.g., "this is fictional" or, in our case, "this is a true biographical sketch"). Finally, genre may convey what convictions the author wishes to produce in the reader. In the case of bios, the author wishes to elicit pattern-imitation of the hero's moral virtues.

The general form of narrative discourse causes the reader to be taken into a story (indirect presentation) rather than confronting him/her with propositional statements (as in the New Testament letters). Narrative discourses contain structural indicators such as "sandwich" patterns and repetitions, summaries, and transition statements. These markers organize the presentation and lend emphasis to key points. Complemented by noting plots and sub-plots in the unfolding narrative, we are then able to

19

formulate the chief purpose of Mark's Gospel. Tracing the flow of thought within such a structured text provides a plausible rationale for the sequences of concepts and connections.

Combining narrative structure, outline, plot, purpose, and analysis of the flow of thought, we will observe that Mark seeks to present Jesus as a teacher and master with great power (in the first part of the Gospel), who is severely tested to the point of death (in the second part of the Gospel). Within this biographical drama, the reader is challenged to side either with the disciples or with the opponents of Jesus, as the general populace recedes more or less into the background. The most prominent factors in the narrative are the self-disclosure of the teacher and the unique and transformative influence the teacher exerts on his pupils (disciples).

Narrative Structure and Outline

Narrative Structure

The New Testament contains four major literary genres: narrative discourses (the Gospels), argumentative discourses (the Epistles and Letters), a historical monograph (Acts), and an apocalyptic text (Revelation).

While argumentative texts express their message in a direct fashion, narrative texts are generally more indirect. Story, setting, time frame, plot, and key figures mark narrative texts, while argumentative texts tend to be much more propositional. Narrative texts generally invite the reader/hearer to participate in what is happening before challenging him/her with a particular message. An Old Testament example of an effective use of narrative is the confrontation of David's adultery (and indirect murder) by Nathan (2 Sam. 12:1–15).

Main structural markers such as headings, summaries, and transition statements are found in the Markan narrative (see, e.g., Mark 1:14–15; 3:7–12; 6:6b; 8:22–26). Further structural markers are the inclusio ("bookends") of the healings of two blind men (Mark 8:22–26; 10:46–52), effectively bracketing the central section of Mark (Mark 8:27–10:45). A conspicuous element in the section 8:27–10:52 is the fact that each of the three predictions of Jesus' passion and resurrection (8:31; 9:31; 10:32–34) is followed by an instruction in discipleship (8:34–38; 9:32–50; 10:35–45). Finally, the conspicuous structural feature of insertions ("sandwiching") has been identified in Mark.[1] Especially when key themes such as discipleship and faith arise, Mark will interrupt a narrative by inserting another pericope and then return to the previous subject (see Mark 3:20–21, 22–30, 31–35; 4:1–9, 10–13, 14–20; and especially 14:1–2, 3–9, 10–11; 14:17–21, 22–26, 27–31; 14:53–54, 55–65, 66–72). James Edwards contends that the inserted pericope holds the key (especially by way of illustration or contrast) to the interpretive purpose of the entire A-B-A unit: "the insertion interprets the flanking halves."[2] These (and other) analyses lead to the following outline of Mark.

Outline[3]

The outline of Mark takes as its starting point the ostensible bipartite structure of the Gospel (with 8:22–26 as a transition section). As stated above, part one concerns the expansive presentation and part two the test and affirmation of Jesus' authority and power. What follows is a combined literary, thematic, and geographical outline.

Introduction, 1:1–15

Part I: Demonstration of Jesus' authority, 1:16–8:26
    1. Work in Galilee, 1:16–3:12
        a. Call of disciples/healing, 1:16–1:45
        b. Enduring in conflict, 2:1–3:12
        Transition, 3:7–12

---

1. James Edwards, "Markan Sandwiches: The Significance of Interpolations in Markan Narratives," *Novum Testamentum* 31, 3 (1989): 193–216.
2. Ibid., 196.
3. This outline is fairly close to that of Eduard Schweizer, "Mark's Theological Achievement," in *The Interpretation of Mark*, ed. W. R. Telford (Edinburgh: T&T Clark, 1995 [1985]), 63–87.

2. Climax in Galilee, 3:13–6:6
    a. Calling of the Twelve, 3:13–35
    b. Parables, 4:1–34
    c. Nature miracle and healing, 4:35–5:43
    d. Lack of faith, 6:1–6
    Transition, 6:6b
3. Work beyond Galilee, 6:7–8:26
    a. Sending of the Twelve, 6:7–13
    b. Death of the Baptist/miracle, 6:14–56
    c. An unclean heart defiles, 7:1–23
    d. Healing/opening to Gentiles, 7:24–30
    e. Decapolis/deafness, 7:31–8:10
    f. Region around Caesarea Philippi/blindness,
       8:11–26
    Transition, 8:22–26

Part II: Testing Jesus' authority in suffering, 8:27–16:8 [9–20]
    4. Caesarea Philippi/journey to Jerusalem, 8:27–10:52
        a. Peter's confession; first passion prediction, 8:27–33
        b. Call to discipleship, 8:34–38
        c. Transfiguration/healing/faith, 9:1–29
        d. Second passion prediction/discipleship, 9:30–50
        e. Instruction/third passion prediction/discipleship,
           10:1–52
        Transition, 10:46–52
    5. Work in Jerusalem, 11:1–13:37
        a. Entry into Jerusalem/cleansing of temple, 11:1–19
        b. Instruction/authority of Jesus, 11:20–12:44
        c. Jesus and the future, 13:1–37
    6. Section: Passion and resurrection in Jerusalem,
       14:1–16:8
        a. Betrayal, 14:1–52
        b. Hearing/sentencing, 14:53–15:20
        c. Crucifixion/empty tomb, 15:21–16:8
        d. [Resurrection appearances, 16:9–14]
        e. [Sending of disciples/ascension, 16:15–20]

Plot and Purpose

Plot

Now that we have traced basic structural and ordering markers of the text, we can complement these observations by noting key stages in narrative discourses.[4] The plot development includes the following:

Stage 1: Description of the Situation, 1:1–15

Stage 2: The Rise of Tension, 1:16–6:6
    Stage 2a—The Beginning of Tension, 1:16–3:12
    Stage 2b—The Concrete Demarcation of Tension,
    3:13–6:6

Stage 3: Increase of Tension, 6:7–13:37
    Stage 3a—The Increase of Tension, 6:7–8:26
    Stage 3b—The Consolidation of Tension, 8:27–10:52
    Stage 3c—The Intensifying Tension, 11:1–13:37

Stage 4: Climax of Tension, 14:1–15:47

Stage 5: Resolution of Tension and Outcome, 16:1–8[9–20].

Identifying major story lines as well as characters arising in the story aids in further isolating the central plot of Mark. The bios genre of Mark already points in this direction: the narrative goal of the Gospel is to present the significant death of its key figure with its ensuing call to discipleship. Telford identifies Jesus, the disciples, and the Jewish leaders as major characters, while many minor characters (including the "people") also play roles in Mark's narrative.[5] The plot arises from tracing the dynamic relationship between Jesus and his disciples (Jesus as the relentless initiator), as well as the climactic conflict between Jesus and his opponents (see also the repeated tension between Jesus and his immediate

---

4. For further details, see below, "The Flow of Thought."
5. W. R. Telford, *Mark* (Sheffield: Sheffield Academic Press, 1995), 108–15.

family). The questions of "who is this Jesus" and "what are his intentions" thus become crystallized in the process. Only Jesus' crucifixion and resurrection clarify these two questions.

Thus far, we have explored the narrative structure, outline, and plot of the Gospel. These various literary elements convey the fact that Mark is a carefully drafted account, containing a simple, straightforward outline and storyline, displaying conspicuous structural elements for emphasis and explanation. A composite of these observations provides the basis for describing the purpose of Mark.

Purpose

Based on these observations, the ultimate purpose of Mark is to legitimize Jesus' universal and authoritative call to discipleship (see the narrative repetition of this theme and the fact that the audience of Jesus splits into followers and opponents as the narrative unfolds). The two-fold outline presented above demonstrates that the central effort in presenting this call is to narrate the identity, action, teaching, and severe testing of Jesus. This fact already indicates that discipleship in Mark is essentially a function of the eminence of the Master's person, deeds, and teaching, not of a certain code of conduct for the disciples.

The Flow of Thought

Keeping the organizing narrative structure, outline, plot, and purpose of Mark in mind, we are now in a position to trace in more detail the Gospel's development of thought and to provide a rationale for its sequence. The following analysis of the flow of thought is set within the general context of the formal analyses provided above.

Part 1: Mark 1:16–8:26—Demonstration of Jesus' Authority

The first half of the Gospel is dedicated to the demonstration of Jesus' expanding authority over sickness, laws of nature, and the demonic world. This is also expressed by his calling, appointing, and sending out his disciples while regularly teaching in a unique and authoritative way.

Mark 1:1–15—Introduction. Plot Development: Stage 1—Description of the Situation. As is the case in some films, the chief character of the story is introduced as one arising from a multitude of people. In this case, the Jewish masses are streaming to the Jordan in response to the Baptist's call to repentance. In succinct succession, Mark presents the Baptist as the herald of a coming One, the baptism of Jesus, and his temptation. All of this leads to the first summary of Jesus' own call to repentance and his teaching on the nearness of the kingdom (or rule) of God in 1:14–15, which in turn commences the report of the public ministry of Jesus.

Mark 1:16–3:12—Work in Galilee. Plot Development: Stage 2a—The Beginning of Tension. The initial calling of disciples, exorcism, healing, and the urgency to preach (Mark 1:16–45; see the summary statement in 3:7–12) all converge to display the unusual authority of Jesus. This theme continues when he boldly and directly forgives the sins of a healed leper, commencing the theme of opposition to Jesus on the part of the spiritual and political leadership of Israel (see especially 2:7).[6] Jesus boldly challenges the cultural and religious convention of the day by conspicuously and intentionally associating with despised tax collectors and "sinners," thereby displaying a clear sense of mission (2:13–17).

A first veiled prediction of Jesus' violent death is found in the metaphor of the bridegroom who is "taken away," thus furnishing a Christ-centered cause for fasting (2:19–20). Together with the section concerning the Sabbath, Mark 2:18–3:6 expresses

---

6. The theme of *opposition* will continue. The Pharisees, Sadducees, and Herodians pursue a policy of preserving their political, economic, and religious power. Judas will oppose Jesus on account of his own openness to Satan and his disappointment over Jesus. Judas had a different plan for Jesus, a different ideology. Peter will deny Jesus in order to preserve his own life. Throughout the various forms of opposition to Jesus, the constant theme is self versus Jesus.

the authority of Jesus over fasting and Sabbath-keeping. While neither fasting nor Sabbath-keeping is rejected, Jesus (re-) injects a consistent God-centered dimension into the two spiritual disciplines. These bold steps and teachings arouse astonishment as well as opposition, causing some to be intent on killing him (3:6).

Mark 3:13–6:6—Climax in Galilee. Plot Development: Stage 2b—The Concrete Demarcation of Tension. A second stage in Jesus' relationship with his disciples is reached when he singles out a distinct group of twelve, who are to form his inner circle. The Twelve are to be with Jesus and to be prepared to help spread the message and exorcise demons, following his example in word and deed (Mark 3:13–19). The foundations of the eternal messianic people of God are thus laid. Opposition comes from his natural family (3:20–21, 31–35) and the spiritual leadership of Israel (3:22–30). Both as a sign of imminent judgment to those on the "outside" and as a means of pedagogical instruction of his disciples, we find Jesus using the rhetorical form of parables. The kingdom (or rule) of God is characterized as his initiating new and redeemed life, that stands in conflict with the powerful and established principles of a God-opposing life. The growth of this new messianic rule is, at first, inconspicuous (4:1–34). Jesus continues to display before his disciples and others his expanding range of power: power over the laws and forces of nature (4:35–41), power over the demonic world (5:1–20), as well as power over human illness and death (5:21–43). Nevertheless, Jesus' reputation in his hometown of Nazareth suffers, being opposed by lack of trust in his divine calling (6:1–6). Similar to the concluding section of 2:1–3:12 (namely, 3:1–6), the section 3:13–6:6 (6:6b summary statement) closes in 6:1–6 once more with the theme of the rejection of Jesus.

Mark 6:7–8:26—Sending Out of the Disciples/Work beyond Galilee/Death of the Baptist/Opening to Gentiles/Warnings. Plot Development: Stage 3a—The Increase of Tension. Jesus' discipleship dynamic reaches a third level as he sends his pupils out in pairs to preach repentance, to exorcise, and to heal (Mark 6:12, 30). The death of the Baptist casts an ominous and telling shadow on Jesus' own destiny (cf. 3:1–6; 6:1–6). Jesus' life is in danger, partially on account of his authoritative, miraculous deeds, partially on account of his extraordinary claims.

Public theories about the increasingly well-known Jesus abound. Herod Antipas, who had ordered the execution of the Baptist, believes Jesus to be the revived Baptist (6:16). The feeding of the five thousand and Jesus' walking on the water continue his display of power (6:31–56). Opposition arises over the proper interpretation of the law of Moses. According to Jesus, focus on the ritual laws of cleanliness at the expense of a renewed heart usurps the purpose of the law and of God himself. On account of the profound defilement of the heart, even the Word of God is anthropocentrically reinterpreted and annulled for personal gain. Without renewed hearts all else is in vain (7:1–23). This radical teaching runs parallel to the continuing display of Jesus' power to cast out demons, to heal, and to multiply food (7:24–8:10). His initial call goes out to the ancient people of Israel. Nevertheless, he already hints at a future ministry of the disciples to Gentiles (7:24–30).

The disbelief of the Jewish leaders (8:11–13) becomes an object lesson for the disciples by means of the metaphor of "leaven" (8:14–21). The disciples do not understand (8:17, 21) or "see" or "hear" (8:18) correctly. This exhortation is reinforced by the contextual echoes of the healing of the deaf mute (7:32–35) and the two-stage healing of the blind man (8:22–26; cf. the "sandwich" of 8:22–26 and 10:46–52). These healings are messianic acts of mercy and, in combination with Jesus' direct warnings (8:17, 18, 21), serve as tools of exposing the hearts of the disciples. The disciples are internally "deaf" and "blind"; they lack true understanding when it comes to "seeing" their own unbelief and tackling the serious problem of their misconception of Jesus. Even in his presence their alertness is at best that of the half-healed blind man who "perceives people as trees moving about" (8:24). This dull perception of themselves and of Jesus extends to Peter's confession of him as Messiah (8:29). The deeply engrained and virtually exclusive focus on the messianic expectation of a Davidic King, devoid of the themes of the suffering Servant/Son of Man and exalted Son of Man, prevent the disciples from seeing: (a) who Jesus really is in both his humility and full splendor and, consequently, (b) who they are in their desperate need of a renewed heart before God. Finally, Mark 8:22–26 serves as a transition to the second half of Mark.

Part 2: Mark 8:27–16:8—Testing of Jesus' Authority in Suffering

The second half of the Gospel narrates the necessity of Jesus' suffering as well as the cost of following the Master. It culminates in the ultimate test of Jesus' astonishing claims and actions: his crucifixion and divine vindication. This will mark the disciples in their fundamental self-understanding and their grasp of the mission of God through Jesus.

Mark 8:27–10:52—Caesarea Philippi/Journey to Jerusalem. Plot Development: Stage 3b—The Consolidation of Tension. The three predictions of Jesus' death and resurrection (8:31; 9:31; 10:32–34) are each followed by instruction on the cost and nature of discipleship.

Jesus now embarks on a course of modifying the disciples' perception of him (and thus their state before God) by means of the relatively uncommon term "Son of Man." In due course, Jesus expands their narrow political perception of the expected Messiah both in terms of a suffering (8:31) and an atoning Son of Man (10:45), as well as an exalted, divine Son of Man (8:38; 14:62; with reference to Dan. 7:13–14). Following each major prediction of the death and resurrection of the Son of Man (Mark 8:31; 9:31; 10:32–34), we find general instructions concerning discipleship. In 8:34–38 the instructions concern "letting go" to be at Jesus' disposal. In 9:33–50 they concern humility and childlike trust. In 10:35–45 they concern humility and servant-hood, culminating in Jesus' own calling to substitutionary atonement (10:45). Jesus' transfiguration (9:2–8) affords a glimpse into his enduring divine nature. It is followed by continued struggle against evil (demons and opposition). The weapons against this evil are prayer (and fasting, 9:29). While less emphasized in the second half of the Gospel, exorcism (9:14–28) and healing (10:46–52) still undergird Jesus' teaching. He also answers questions concerning marriage (10:1–12) and addresses the serious conflict between material wealth and entry into God's kingdom (10:17–31).

Mark 11:1–13:37—Work in Jerusalem. Plot Development: Stage 3c—The Intensifying Tension. Jesus enters Jerusalem triumphantly, cleanses the temple, and teaches both opponents and disciples authoritatively.

Jesus' entry into Jerusalem (11:1–11) temporarily permits the prominence of Davidic royal connotations of his messianic identity (11:10). Jesus "visits" Jerusalem in humility and zeal for the true worship of God. The cursing of the fig tree and the cleansing of the temple stand in sharp antithesis to trust in God, which brings forth fruit (11:12–25). Rejection of Jesus and unbelief go hand in hand (11:27–12:12). Opposition grows, despite the fact that Jesus cannot be convicted of breaking the law of Moses (cf. 12:13–37: on marriage, on the chief commandment, and on "David's Lord"). In sharp contrast to his proud and exploiting opponents, Jesus praises the sacrificial devotion of a poor widow (12:38–44). The eschatological prospect concludes Jesus' instructions with a focus on being alert to God's will and ways in the midst of imminent (regional) and future (cosmic) calamities (13:1–37). Readiness to suffer and to trust is central for his followers.

Mark 14:1–15:47—Passion in Jerusalem. Plot Development: Stage 4—The Climax of Tension. The passion narrative moves quickly from the celebration of the Passover, Jesus' betrayal, Gethsemane, and his arrest, to Jesus' trials before the Sanhedrin and Pilate. It climaxes in Jesus' crucifixion and the discovery of the empty tomb, complemented by the messenger's announcement of Jesus' resurrection.

The passion of Jesus is described in a focused manner and runs essentially parallel to Matthew and Luke. While Jesus has displayed his power in many ways, he now faces the ultimate test of his claims and actions. The betrayal narrative (14:1–52) introduces this ultimate test. The pericope leading up to the celebration of the Last Supper (14:12–26) contains a last reference to the opponents' intent to have Jesus executed (14:1–1). Mark 14:25–26 concludes the narrative of the Passover meal, followed by the prediction of Peter's denial of Jesus (14:27–31; cf. 14:66–72) and Jesus' prayer in the garden of Gethsemane (14:32–42). Mark 14:42 concludes the account of Jesus' fellowship with his disciples prior to his death.

Now that Jesus has unmistakably identified himself before the Sanhedrin and the high priest as the eternal Son of God and the exalted Son of Man (14:62; cf. Dan. 7:13–14; Ps. 110:1, 5), final preparations for his execution following the verdict of blasphemy (and the trial before Pilate) push relentlessly forward (15:1–20). The crucifixion itself is told in very terse terms. Those who oppose and mock Jesus speak and act prior to his death (15:21–38). Those who admire or believe and follow Jesus are mentioned subsequent to his death (15:39–47).

Mark 16:1–8 [9–20]—Testimony to the Resurrection. Plot Development: Stage 5—Resolution of Tension and Outcome. While none of the actual resurrection appearances (cf. 1 Cor. 15 and other passages) are recorded in Mark, the messenger of God speaks of Jesus' resurrection (Mark 16:6) to the women who had followed him. The empty tomb is part of the fulfillment of Jesus' prediction of his resurrection (8:31 and elsewhere).

The longer ending of Mark (16:8–20) contains reports of Jesus' postresurrection appearances. It also narrates his Great Commission and speaks of faith, miracles, and evangelism.[7]

7. Regarding the difficult, text-critical issues surrounding the original ending of Mark, see, e.g., William L. Lane, *The Gospel of Mark*, NICNT (Grand Rapids: Eerdmans, 1974), 591–92; 601–5. See also David Alan Black, ed., *Perspectives on the Ending of Mark* (Nashville: Broadman and Holman, 2008).

Conclusion

We stated above that, at least in antiquity, form served content. Our analysis of the structure of Mark, its outline, narrative plot, purpose, and flow of thought thus aids in hearing its overall message.

The genre of ancient biography already conveys the author's intent, namely, that he seeks to present a true-to-life witness account of a historical person and intends to elicit a form of imitation from readers. This claim is reinforced by the historical plausibility that Jesus systematically taught his disciples to remember his deeds and words.

The narrative discourse with its structure and plot allows readers to enter the unfolding drama, helps them to relive the increasing tension and ultimate resolution of the drama, and challenges them to make moral judgments. In Mark's account these decisions focus on taking sides either with Jesus' disciples or with his opponents, as the public recedes into the background.

As we consider Mark's narrative structure, outline, plot, and analysis of its flow of thought,[8] we note that he presents Jesus as a powerful teacher (first half of the account) who is nevertheless severely tested to the point of death (second half of the account). The most significant elements in the narrative are the self-disclosure of the teacher and the unique, transformative influence he exerts on his pupils.

Based on the formal observations presented above, we have come to the conclusion that the ultimate purpose of Mark is to present, legitimize, and describe Jesus' universal and authoritative call to discipleship. The central effort in legitimizing this call is to narrate the identity, action, teaching, and severe testing of Jesus. The ultimate legitimization is Jesus' resurrection. This observation already indicates that discipleship in Mark is essentially a function of the eminence of the Master's

---

8. The analysis of the flow of thought gives a *rationale* for the interconnection of the small and large units of such a narrative.

person, deeds, teaching, and impact; discipleship is not primarily a matter of pursuing a certain code of conduct. The form of Mark's account thus already suggests that fellowship with Jesus (including dependence upon his atonement), confessing him, and being marked by his conduct make up the heart of discipleship, resulting in transformed persons who then also act differently (pattern-imitation). Discipleship thus promises to be profoundly Christ-centered.

Mark's Thematic Framework: The In-Breaking of God's Eternal Rule

JESUS' TEACHING on the kingdom of God constitutes the overall thematic context within which questions concerning his own identity and the call to ongoing discipleship arise. It is in the context of the dawning of the messianic rule of God that Jesus confronts the disciples with two core questions: "Who do you perceive yourself to be?" and "Who do you perceive God to be?"

We must, therefore, seek to understand the mission that God undertook in his eternal kingdom by sending his eternal Son. Before we turn to our central interest in tracing the nature and effect of Jesus' call to discipleship in Mark, then, we will briefly consider his teaching on the messianic kingdom of God. In essence, Jesus' announcement of the messianic rule of God challenges human self-will and autonomy. It marks the announcement of God's claim on his creation.

Various Expectations of the Kingdom of God at the Time of Jesus

Parallel to the different expectations of the Messiah—the Messiah of God vs. popular, political, Davidic expectations—there are differences between popular expectations of the kingdom of God in Palestinian Judaism and Jesus' teaching on the subject.

In the minds of most first-century A.D. Jews, the coming kingdom of God was primarily to be realized by the reestablishment of a Jewish theocracy in Palestine following liberation from Roman suppression. This theocracy would be administered by a Davidic King. The blueprint for such expectations was the Jewish Maccabean uprising against the Seleucid Syrian powers, especially against Antiochus Epiphanes IV in the second century B.C. There were also alternate apocalyptic expectations of the kingdom of God. These envisioned a new era following the judgment and destruction of the present era.

Both political (popular) and apocalyptic (less popular) perspectives in Palestinian Judaism at the time of Jesus unite in their understanding that a new age follows the old, present age (cf. Matt. 3:1–12; 12:32).

The Old Testament Background to Jesus' Teaching on the Kingdom of God

While the phrase "kingdom of God" is rarely used in the Old Testament,[1] the concept of the kingly rule and power of God is, nevertheless, widely represented.

1. God is known as ruler over his creation (cf. Pss. 29:10; 47:6–9; 95:3; 103:10, 19; 145:13; Isa. 6:5; 24:21ff.; Jer. 10:10; 46:18).
2. In redemptive history, God is the sole Lord of his people (cf. Exod. 15:18; 19:6; Pss. 10:16; 29:10; 114:7; Isa. 24:23; 43:15; Jer. 31:31–34; Zech. 14:1–10; Obad. 1:21). This holds true even when he is represented by various judges, priests, prophets, and kings (Deut. 18:15, 18; Isa. 9:11; Jer. 33:15–16; Ezek. 11:17; 34:23ff.; Amos 9:11, 13–15).

1. See George E. Ladd, *The Gospel of the Kingdom* (Grand Rapids: Eerdmans, 1959), 230–38.

In Psalm 2, as well as 2 Samuel 7:11–16 (cf. Mic. 4:1–5; Isa. 2:12–17; 35:4–5, 10; 40:1–11; 53:1–12; Jer. 30:4–9; Ezek. 37:26ff.; Dan. 2:36–45) we find political and transcendent, present and future elements which are only connected by the coming of Christ.[2]

Contrary to the above-mentioned narrow and popular expectations in first century A.D. Palestine, Jesus teaches the kingdom of God as the fulfillment of a large and diverse body of Old Testament prophecy.

Some Characteristic Features of Jesus' Teaching on the Kingdom of God

Jesus' teaching on the nearness of the kingdom of God signals a shift of perspective away from human expectations to God's view and interpretation of the world. At its core, Jesus announces that God's will and sovereign rule will again become paramount to human life across the globe. The announcement of the messianic kingdom of God signals a fundamental challenge to human autonomy and outright enmity toward God's place in the universe. Human independence and God's sovereign rule cannot, in the end, coexist. One of these forces has to yield. Jesus' call to repent and surrender is thus to be seen in the advancing messianic kingdom of God.

The message of the rising messianic kingdom of God represents God's overall interpretation of—and approach to—the ills and the remedies for human life on earth.

God's People

Jesus' teaching concerning the kingdom of God (cf. Mark 1:15; 9:1; 14:25; 15:43) clearly implies the anticipation that God is

2. Cf. Ladd, *Gospel of the Kingdom*, 230–38; Geerhardus Vos, *Biblical Theology* (Grand Rapids: Eerdmans, 1948), 372.

continuing to call a particular people unto himself. The people of God are now, however, drawn from the entire world and are no longer confined to a geographically limited theocracy.[3] The people of God now consist of Jewish ("holy remnant," Rom. 9–11) and Gentile believers. God calls, in continuation of Israel, a world-wide, messianic people (Mark 13:10). The exalted Jesus is eternally enthroned on the messianic throne of David (Acts 2:30).

The New Era Arises during the Time of the Old Era

The kingdom and rule of God begin now as the new era arises within—and concurrent to—the old era (Luke 4:21/Isa. 61:1–2; Matt. 11:2–6/Isa. 35:5–6). This is a genuine eschatological event. It will culminate in the last Judgment and endure forever (cf. John 18:36).

As with the other Gospels, Mark conveys both present[4] (Mark 1:15; 10:14, 15, 23, 24, 25; 12:34; cf. Luke 11:20; 16:16; 17:20–21; Matt. 11:13; 12:28 ff.; 13:16) and future, universally visible, aspects of God's kingdom (Mark 9:47–48; 14:25; Matt. 6:10; 25:34; Luke 16:19–31; 19:11). At times, both present and future aspects might be in view (Mark 4:11, 26, 30; cf. the temporally neutral expression in 15:43). The present commencement of God's messianic rule includes the overcoming of Satan (Matt. 12:29).

Repentance as Condition for Entry into the Messianic Kingdom

Repentance and forgiveness through Jesus are thus closely associated with the coming of the kingdom of God (Mark 4:12; cf. 1:14–15/Isa. 52:7). In this way the disciples are to "enter" or "receive" the kingdom (Mark 4; Matt. 13; Luke 8; as well as Matt. 6:33; 11:11; Luke 7:28; 18:17).

---

3. Compare Acts 1:6 with 1:8 and 3:21. See also Rom. 4:13: Abraham is the "heir of the world."

4. See John Calvin, *Institutes of the Christian Religion*, trans. Ford Lewis Battles, ed. John McNeil (Philadelphia: Westminster John Knox Press, 1960), 1.5.25, which states: "By announcing the Kingdom of God, he called for faith, since by the Kingdom of God which he declared to be at hand, he meant forgiveness of sins, salvation, life, and every blessing which we obtain in Christ."

Jesus' teaching concerning the kingdom is a public description of the coming Messiah who personally calls to discipleship. Jesus lives and teaches in order to call people into discipleship and thus to return them to a life under the eternal, life-giving, and direct rule of God.[5] We note the close connection between Jesus' teaching on the "kingdom of God," "salvation," and "eternal life" in Mark 10: "eternal life" (10:17, 30; so often in the Gospel of John); "salvation" (10:26), and "entry into the kingdom of God" (10:23, 24, 25; cf. John 3:3, 5).

The Kingdom in Jesus' Parables

The Kingdom's Inconspicuous Beginning and Great End. The messianic kingdom of God begins modestly and inconspicuously (cf. 4:26)[6] but moves toward a triumphant, universal goal. Where Jesus is, there the eternal, messianic kingdom has already begun.

The Kingdom's Inviting Father and Judge. The kingdom parables present God as Father (cf. Matt. 6:26; Luke 12:32) and as the one who invites (Matt. 22:1ff.; Luke 14:16ff.; Luke 15; cf. 2:15–17). They also present him as the one who judges (Matt. 25:34, 41). The three kingdom parables in Mark 4 contain the common thread that God works directly toward the growth of his kingdom. The parable of the sower describes the Word of God, especially Jesus' life and work, which bears the fruit of reconciliation, worship, and witness. The parable of the self-growing seed describes the fact that God causes growth (maturity in following Christ). The parable of the mustard seed emphasizes the fact that despite very modest beginnings there is a glorious end in sight.

The Relationship between the Kingdom of God and the Messiah of God

A further unique aspect of Jesus' teaching on the subject is the fact that he connects the true kingdom of God and the

---

5. Vos, *Biblical Theology*, 387.
6. Ibid., 374.

Messiah of God. He does this by implying that he is the sacrificial inaugurator (in the death of the Son of Man) and the eternal King (Lord) of that kingdom. All of these elements testify to the fact that the Son of God is laying the foundation for the eternal messianic kingdom of God (cf. Mark 12:10): the divine necessity of the death of the Son of Man (8:31; Luke 12:49–50), the assurance of his vindication and resurrection (Mark 9:31; 10:35–45), the saving significance of his death (2:10f; 10:45), and the reference to the new covenant in his blood (14:24).

Despite his impending death, Jesus declares that he will be the leader (*pater familias*) of the future messianic banquet (14:25).

Conclusion

In summary, we can state that Jesus' teaching about the messianic rule of God anticipates that the government of God's people will be returned to God himself—the Messiah will turn out to be the eternal Son of God. However, Jesus does not thereby reject concrete Old Testament prophecies concerning the messianic rule on earth. Rather, this rule is broadened to the prophesied universal dimension (e.g., Isa. 42:1, 4, 6 and 49:6). The kingdom is to be expected on earth but not mediated by a mere human (such as David). Rather, the incarnate Son of God, fulfilling human and divine aspects of Old Testament kingdom expectations, eternally rules as messianic King over his people worldwide.

Part 2

The Dynamic between God's Messiah and Authentic Disciples

Witness to the Unique
Person of Jesus

WE HAVE SEEN that Jesus' message of the kingdom of God means nothing less than that God is taking up his own direct rule over his people. Jesus' teaching anticipates the fulfillment of Old Testament prophecy by means of a human and divine Messiah who will govern the people of God. We will now trace Mark's testimony to the complex and intriguing figure of Jesus.

Mark testifies to the fact that Jesus is the eternal Son of God who dies a substitutionary death by crucifixion. Jesus' purpose is to rule over his people based on his humiliation, sacrifice, and reconciling work. He thereby establishes a discipleship movement that grows in utter dependence upon this eternal, divine, and human Messiah-King.

As mentioned previously, many contemporary scholars believe that Mark's account represents merely a faith-projection of the early church and is not a witness to the true Jesus. For example, Ludwig Feuerbach, who influenced Karl Marx, claimed that all religion is mere psychological projection. According to Feuerbach, human beings fix their transcendent hopes on some immanent object. In the case of Christianity, the object of faith-projections is the simple, merely human preacher Jesus of Nazareth.

What is noteworthy, however, is the fact that Mark portrays the disciples in a very different light. They know who they are looking for from the start. They know how the Messiah is to look and act.

They have a fixed set of expectations and scriptural interpretations, taught for centuries by synagogue teachers all over Israel. What is so disarming and indicative of the authenticity of the account is that Jesus radically deconstructs these predetermined expectations and interpretations. Mark's account exposes in a most honest way the disciples' wrong attitudes and expectations. The witness to Jesus thus occurs against the background of their shattered messianic expectations, not as a filling out of their faith-projections. Jesus deconstructs their self-assurance and their fixed belief system and restores them to personal trust in the one triune God. He does this without reinterpreting the Old Testament but rather by re-establishing the full force and claim of the Old Testament.

Far from being a mere faith-projection, the discipleship dynamic centers on Jesus' radically challenging self-disclosure and his exposure of the disciples' misguided beliefs about themselves and God. Parallel to this counterintuitive truth claim of Mark's account we thus note Jesus' profound personal challenge to the disciples. And since the dynamic relationship between the disciples and Jesus is essentially a function of Jesus' identity, a study of the person of Jesus directly shapes the character of discipleship. We must explore, therefore, who Jesus reveals himself to be in order to trace his impact on his disciples.

Various Messianic Expectations at the Time of Jesus

The Davidic, Political Messianic Ruler

It is clear that popular Judaism at the time of Jesus expected a Davidic, political messianic ruler who would liberate the Jewish people from Roman suppression and defilement. Other messianic expectations at the time of Jesus have been documented,[1] but they do not represent a widespread, popular view. Jesus challenges

---

1. The expectations of a priestly Messiah (1QS 9, 11; 4Q 175; CD 7), an anointed prophet (PsSal 17 and 18), or a heavenly Son of Man (Eth. Enoch 37–71) exist on the periphery of first-century Judaism. See John J. Collins, *The Scepter and the Star: Messiahs of the Dead Sea Scrolls and Other Ancient Literature* (New Haven, CT: Anchor Bible Books, 1995), 209.

the popular view held by the disciples. He presents a messianic expectation that includes more of the Old Testament than the narrow, politicized popular messianic expectation surrounding 2 Samuel 7:12–14. He presents a messianic spectrum of humiliation-exaltation (Isa. 53; Dan. 7:13–14) that is unique to himself.

The danger of forcing Jesus into the role of a narrowly defined, political, quasi-religious guerrilla leader against the Roman Empire, like those of the Maccabean uprising, was real and substantial (cf. Luke 24:21; Acts 1:6). John's Gospel features the serendipitous and telling remark, "Jesus, knowing that they intended to come and make him king by force, withdrew again to a mountain by himself" (John 6:15).

We notice in Jesus' teaching a corrective element with regard to the messianic expectation of the disciples and Palestinian Judaism in general. The messianic strand of the Servant of God (*Ebed Yahweh*; see 2:20; Isa. 53:8) finds its place here. The theme of the rejection of the Messiah (Mark 8:31/10:45) is of great import. According to Jesus, the exaltation of the Messiah of God (14:62; Ps. 110:1, 5; Dan. 7:13–14) is to be preceded by a period of extreme humiliation and suffering (Isa. 53; Mark 10:45; 14:25). There is thus a clash between the suffering (and highly exalted) Messiah of God on the one hand and the political messianic expectations in first-century Palestinian Judaism on the other. This clash necessitates Jesus' own "messianic secret," whereby he must require silence of the disciples on this issue until his resurrection (9:9). In other words, Jesus has to navigate the difficult path of rejecting narrow political messianic expectations (John 6:15) while at the same time affirming all biblical messianic truths (Mark 8:30; 9:9).

The Historical Messianic Secret

Oscar Cullmann and others[2] have attempted to give a historical explanation for the need of a messianic secret:

2. Oscar Cullmann, *Christology* (Louisville: Westminster John Knox, 1959), ad loc.; Ralph Martin, *Mark: Evangelist and Theologian* (Carlyle, UK: Paternoster, 1972); James Dunn, "The Messianic Secret in Mark," *Tyndale Bulletin* 21 (1970): 92–117.

- There is an element of secrecy (cf. Mark 7:24; 8:30; 9:9, 30) in the very fact that God's Messiah had to die and be raised from death in order to be enthroned as the eternal Messiah-ruler (Acts 2:36). There was, therefore, an element of anticipation of this necessary event during the life of Jesus (cf. Mark 9:9 in this light).[3]
- Jack Kingsbury[4] has convincingly argued that there is thus a corrective element with regard to the messianic identity of Jesus over against the messianic expectation of the disciples (and Palestinian Judaism in general). The heightened expectation for the Messiah among Jews, especially the Pharisees, in the first half of the first century narrowed Old Testament messianic expectations (see the focus on 2 Sam. 7:12–14, 16; 4Q Flor 1, 11–13). This expectation clashed with the messianic identity and mission of Jesus. It is thus necessary for Jesus to issue injunctions of silence to his disciples until they grasp what the mission of God's Messiah is, which includes his suffering and death. This also explains the motif for the disciples' lack of understanding.
- The injunctions to silence toward the demons are necessary on spiritual grounds as the demons misuse the truth.
- The injunctions to silence toward healed persons are necessary on political grounds and are connected with the second point above.

Wrede's Unconvincing Alternative

The messianic secrecy motif in Mark has been a major topic of discussion since the publication of William Wrede's *The Messianic Secret* in 1901.[5] Wrede lumps together three distinctive motifs found in Mark:

3. Bar-Cochba as a messianic contender had to be confirmed by his life.
4. Jack Dean Kingsbury, *Christology* (Minneapolis: Fortress Press, 1983), 11–15, 21, 136, 147.
5. Wilhelm Wrede, *The Messianic Secret*, rev. ed., trans. J. C. G. Greig (Greenwood, SC/Cambridge, MA: Attic Press/James Clarke, 1971).

1. Jesus' injunctions of silence to demons (Mark 1:23–24; 3:11–12; 5:6–7), to healed people (1:43–44; 5:43; 7:3b; 8:26), and to his disciples (8:30; 9:9);
2. secrecy surrounding Jesus (7:24; 9:30); and
3. the disciples' lack of understanding (8:17ff. ; 8:31–33; 9:9–13; 9:31–32; 10:34 ff.).

Wrede's ingenious but flawed thesis was that "Mark," an unknown creative theologian at the end of the first century A.D., linked the messianic faith of the early church with the nonmessianic tradition of Jesus by means of his own messianic secrecy idea. "Mark" was thus able to retain both the integrity of the historical tradition (Jesus as a nonmessianic prophet) handed down to him as well as the church's messianic faith (Jesus had supposedly become the object of messianic projections). Wrede held that it was only necessary to historicize the secrecy motif into the life of the historical Jesus as a narrative link between these two (essentially incompatible) strands. For instance, injunctions to silence were placed by "Mark" (8:30) in order to link Jesus' nonmessianic life (8:27–28) with the confession of the early church (a confession placed into Peter's mouth in 8:29).

However, Wrede fails to explain the origin and development of the messianic faith in Jesus, especially in clear contrast to popular messianic expectations. Even though the physical resurrection (which Wrede did not consider a historical fact) does confirm Jesus' messianic claims, it does not constitute his messianic identity. We thus ask: from where did the faith in Jesus as suffering and exalted Messiah arise, if not from his own teaching and the ensuing events?[6] Wrede never answered this question from a historically plausible standpoint; he was satisfied with the sheer postulate that the early church believed in Jesus as Messiah. Furthermore, Wrede never proved the existence of a nonmessianic, pre-Markan Jesus.[7] Finally,

6. It is astonishing how uncritically Wrede's theories have been accepted by "critical" scholarship from Rudolf Bultmann to Heikki Räisänen and Bart Ehrman.

7. Toward the end of his life, Wrede wrote a letter to Adolf von Harnack dated January 2, 1905, stating that he was now more inclined to believe that Jesus considered himself to be the Messiah. See Hans-Josef Rollmann and Werner Zager, "Unveröffentlichte Briefe

Wrede did not pay attention to the fact that the three motifs mentioned by him (see above) are to be sharply distinguished.

Since it can be shown that there exists a plausible historical explanation for the need of a messianic secret in the public life of Jesus, the hypothesis of Wrede has lost its foundation, namely, that the messianic secrecy motif was a literary construction by "Mark."

Conflicting Expectations of the Messiah at the Time of Jesus

The historical need for a messianic secret underscores the historical (religious-political) danger in which God's Messiah found himself. It also highlights the fact that the disciples (together with Palestinian Judaism) did not understand God's Messiah. The fact that Jesus is reported to have repeatedly taught his disciples about this very difference (8:27–33; 9:31; 10:32–34) on account of their lack of understanding speaks further for the existence of the historical messianic secret.

In sum: it is the clash between the perspective of the suffering and highly exalted Messiah of God and the political messianic expectations in first-century Palestinian Judaism that necessitated Jesus' "messianic secret."

In this context, Jesus' injunctions to silence make sense. Imagine the political situation at the time of Jesus to be fuel-enriched air. All you need is a little spark that will start an explosion. The spark may come from someone who claims to be the Messiah-liberator. As the Jewish historian Josephus recounts, there was a heightened expectation of a liberator at the time of Jesus. The danger of "guerilla warfare" and revolution was very high. It can be explained by recourse to the Maccabean uprising in the second century B.C. Then, the Jewish people had been suppressed by various foreign powers, and this uprising sought to free them from oppression. The Maccabean uprising actually led to the re-establishment of Israel's theocracy around 160 B.C. It was seen as the triumph of God to help guerrilla fighters stand

---

William Wredes zur Problematisierung des messianischen Selbstverständnisses Jesu," *Zeitschrift für neuere Theologiegeschichte* 8 (2001): 274–322.

up against a great military power. At the time of Jesus, this uprising served as one of the primary lenses through which the Old Testament was all too often read.

The people of Israel thus had a fixed plan for their Messiah, and the Messiah had to fit into that plan (cf. John 6:15). When we place the very different picture of God's Messiah, Jesus, into that setting, we encounter a nearly unmanageable circumstance. As soon as Jesus acts remotely like the expected messianic figure, he will be the spark which may cause a political uprising. While the atmosphere is pregnant with a particular expectation of political liberation, Jesus, as the eternal Son of God, is sent for a broader messianic purpose that includes the totality of the Old Testament anticipation of liberation by God. That plan does not ignore the plight of the Jewish people at the time of the New Testament, but it has a much deeper and more universal perspective of God's purposes. The root problem of human alienation from God and self has to be dealt with above all else.

For this reason Jesus gives injunctions to silence, when individuals are healed, for instance. He is constantly working in a setting of substantial misunderstanding, and yet he heals and displays mercy. He is constantly straddling the presentation and proclamation of God's intent in a setting in which he can easily be misunderstood. Jesus thus lives in the context of conflicting messianic expectations. It is true that Jesus often says, "Do not speak about it," and then a particular person still goes and tells everybody.[8] The general injunction to silence is necessary. I am convinced that when the people who were healed tell about the great works of God in their lives, it actually limits what Jesus can do.

The Messiah of God

Now that we have described the tension-laden situation in which Jesus made himself known, we ask who God's Messiah is

8. An exception lies in Jesus' initial work in the Decapolis—a non-Jewish Gentile area to the east of the Sea of Galilee—where he tells the healed person to go tell everyone. At a later stage in Jesus' work in the Decapolis, he issues an injunction to silence to another person healed there.

in his full identity and richly diverse functions. Our findings will profoundly shape the answer to our question of what discipleship is all about.

Jesus, the Messiah of God as a Common Human Being

Mark portrays Jesus as a human being full of compassion and mercy (Mark 1:41; 6:34; 8:2) as well as righteous anger and indignation (3:5; 8:33; 10:14); he is distressed by suffering (14:33ff.), experiences emotional fatigue (7:34; 8:12) and hunger (11:12), is in need of sleep (4:38), and experiences astonishment (6:6).

Jesus, the Messiah of God as a Divine Being

However, the disciples are soon confronted with a person who exhibits not only human but also divine characteristics. The divine nature of Jesus becomes apparent in his extraordinary power over nature and demons, in his transfiguration, and in his claims to be the "Son of God," the "Son of Man," and "Lord." Since we have already described Jesus' extraordinary power (see chapter 2), we now turn to an examination of the other characteristics listed here.

The Transfiguration. The transfiguration narrative (9:2–8) offers the divine self-revelation of Jesus as the Son of God. Mark 9:1 identifies the imminent transfiguration as an anticipation of the future kingdom of God.

For a brief time, Jesus displays his full glory to the three disciples present. As we see here the future King, we also see the rule of that King symbolized by the meeting between him, Moses, and Elijah. Moses represents the Torah (Law). Elijah represents the Prophets. The major function of the prophets was to call people back to the ways (Torah) of God. In fact, we can argue that John the Baptist and the apostles were prophetic repentance preachers in the pattern of Old Testament prophets. And as we look at this passage we will be surprised by what Peter intends to do. He will learn something new about the kingdom of God.

It is important to note that the three chief witnesses of the transfiguration are the disciples of Jesus' "inner circle," one of whom, Peter, will later mention the event in 2 Peter 1:16–18 shortly before his martyrdom. This event occurs singularly for the benefit of these three disciples (and, by implication, for us). This becomes apparent in Mark 9:2, 4, 7, and 12. The disciples are to see, hear, and learn through this amazing event.

As Jesus is transfigured, he radiates from the inside out. Note the difference in the radiance of Moses when he receives the Ten Commandments (Exod. 34:29–30, 33, 35). As the sun sheds light on the moon which leads to polarized light, so the glory of God shines on Moses, and he reflects the glory of God when the Jews see him (cf. Matt. 17:1–13). The description here of the radiance of Jesus is different. It corresponds precisely with what is said in Revelation that in the new earth and heavens there will be no need for a sun because the very glory of the Father and the Lamb will be the light (Rev. 21:23; cf. Ezek. 1:22–28). The radiance is described in very interesting terms: "And his clothes became radiant, intensely white, as no one on earth could bleach them" (Mark 9:3). When we encounter comparisons like this, we are confronted with the divine. This is not a secondary, derivative light source but the divine nature of Jesus.

Philippians 2:5–7 repeats this by saying: "Christ Jesus, who, though he was in the form of God, did not count equality with God a thing to be grasped, but made himself nothing, taking the form of a servant." He relinquished divine privileges, existing in the eternal love with the Father and the Holy Spirit, and poured himself out, taking on the confinement of human incarnation, living truly as God and man.

As we contemplate the transfiguration, we see a human being radiating divine glory with supremacy over the great mediator of the law (Moses) and over the prophetic heritage (Elijah). The unique One who is the only Son of the Father is before us. Perhaps we should think of the incarnation as Jesus' self-limitation into human existence in which he is truly tempted as we are, truly hungry as we are, and empathizes with us because he lived a life

49

like ours (Heb. 4:14–15; 5:7–9). The divide between Creator and creature is retained eternally, but as Jesus let go of great glory and privilege to look us in the eye, we are likewise called to serve others in a similar way.

In the midst of this miraculous occurrence Peter intends to build three tabernacles and to stay up on the mountain permanently. He sees Moses, Elijah, and Jesus on the same level. Peter is slow to realize who God's Messiah really is (cf. Acts 1:6).[9] We must notice God's mercy in this account: "And a cloud overshadowed them, and a voice came out of the cloud, 'This is my beloved Son. Listen to him'" (Mark 9:7). This echoes Deuteronomy 18:15, 18: "The LORD your God shall raise up a prophet like [Moses] from among you . . . it is to him you shall listen." The heavenly Father helps shape the understanding of Peter, John, and James regarding the full identity of God's eternal Son. We see here already how truth about Jesus is intimately connected with true discipleship. Peter needs to recognize who it is that pursues him. The Messiah is not like Moses or Elijah. He is the only One who receives the divine affirmation as the eternal Son.

Twice in Mark the heavenly Father affirms Jesus as his Son (Mark 1:11; 9:7; cf. Psalm 2), saying, "You are my beloved Son." There is a great encouragement for the disciples in this affirmation, which is not only the affirmation of Jesus as the eternal Son of God who is well loved by his Father; nor is it only the affirmation of the divine glory of Jesus. There is far more to it than for us to simply understand that he is the exalted Son of Man.

Rather, since we are adopted sons and daughters,[10] believers benefit from—and are included in—the Father's love for his Son. We indeed receive this profound affirmation from God. We have been brought into a family in which every natural and adopted member receives that kind of love. And that inclusion in divine love is based neither on where we come from nor on our performance. Rather, it is based solely on adoption. We have no claim to boast, we have nothing to offer that qualifies us above others.

9. Note, however, Peter's recollection of this event in 2 Peter 1:16–17.
10. See Rom. 8:15, 23; 9:4; Gal. 4:5; Eph. 1:5.

The proper question to ask when we come to God is, "Why did you adopt *me?*" The affirmation of the Father's love for the Son is thus extended to his adopted children.

Mark 9:8 adds a sobering note: "And suddenly, looking around, they no longer saw anyone with them but Jesus only." It is a great comfort that Jesus is still with them. He will go with them to Jerusalem and will do what he said. What he has prophesied about himself will come to pass; he will be vindicated. Later, he will go before them to Galilee. He will appear to them as the resurrected Christ. They will be equipped with the seal of the Holy Spirit in their hearts. Their hope lies in their dependence upon Jesus. As they descend from the mountain, they are confronted with the pain of human existence. They see the stark reality which necessitates the "greater exodus" which Jesus leads.

The mount of transfiguration opens a true window into the identity of him who calls us to follow him. He is alive today. He is the humble Son of Man who has come to us. And he is truly exalted to share, once again, divine glory with the Father and the Spirit (Phil. 2:5–11). This truth will become visible at the God-appointed time. Yet it already defines us now. He is even now shaping us into his followers, just as he did with his first disciples, disarming us so that we, like them, will surrender our self-sufficiency and greed as well as our own plans for the Messiah.

Jesus, the Messiah of God, as the Son of God. The transfiguration of Jesus obviously displays and confirms his divine nature as the heavenly voice declares him the "beloved Son" and calls the disciples to "listen to him" (cf. Deut. 18:15, 18). Unmistakably, the term "Son of God" here is meant in its full sense and not merely as a phrase of adoption. Jesus is eternally Son of the Father, sharing in his divine nature.

According to Vincent Taylor and others, the title Son of God constitutes a central phrase in Mark. Taylor notes the bracket verses of 1:1 and 15:39. Conspicuously placed references to "[my beloved] Son" at Jesus' baptism (1:11), his transfiguration (9:7), and the Parable of the Wicked Husbandmen (12:6–8) are noteworthy

51

as well. So is the fact of Jesus' self-identification as the Son (not even the Son knows "that hour," 13:32). Demons refer to Jesus as "the Son of [the Most High] God" (3:11; 5:7), and the high priest links the Messiah with "the Son of the Blessed" (14:61; probably based on reports about Jesus' claims in 12:1–12). Furthermore, exclusive "Father" references in 8:36 (the Son of Man's Father), 13:32 (the Father who knows the hour), and 14:36 complement this picture.

Jesus, the Messiah of God, as the Son of Man. The phrase "Son of Man" occurs about seventy-two times in the Gospels and always in sayings of Jesus. This phrase is a singular phenomenon in early Christianity because the early church never says, "If you confess Jesus as 'Son of Man' you shall be saved." In fact, the phrase "Son of Man" virtually disappears after the Gospels. There are a few exceptions, notably the stoning of Stephen in Acts 7. Being close to death, Stephen sees the exalted Son of Man standing in the presence of the Almighty Father. Some interpreters note that Jesus is usually viewed as seated at the right hand of the Father. Stephen, however, is being stoned as one of the disciples of Jesus, thus Jesus stands to advocate for him (Acts 7:56). Stephen is given a vision into the reality of the triune God.

The implication of all of this is that "Son of Man" is a unique way in which Jesus refers to himself. Perhaps an analogy would be helpful here: Some spacecraft use booster rockets to launch them into space. Once the booster rocket has done its job, it falls off and plunges to earth. Jesus' use of the phrase "Son of Man" is comparable to such a booster rocket. Once this phrase has "launched" a dynamic understanding of the greatness of the Son of God, it "falls to the ground" and is "collected" by the witnesses as a unique self-designation of Jesus in the Gospels.

Critical scholars have tried to separate Jesus from the concept of the suffering and exalted Son of Man, but this key phrase turns out to be historical bedrock, allowing us access to Jesus' own unique understanding of himself. Three distinct but related ideas can be connected with this phrase.

First, Jesus often uses the term to refer to his humble, human state (a factor more prominent in Matthew and Luke: e.g., "The Son of Man has no place to lay his head," Matt. 8:20). The phrase, at times, simply denotes in Aramaic the circumlocution for the personal pronoun "I."

Second, Jesus' frequent references to the necessity of the Son of Man's sufferings (Mark 8:31; 10:45; 14:21, 36) have caused much debate. No one can doubt that there are historical circumstances which point to the intention of opponents to execute Jesus. There are, for example, no less than fifteen conflict discourses in Mark 1–12 alone. Opposition grows proportionally with Jesus' claims. However, it appears that he employs the relatively uncommon and, for his purposes, useful phrase "Son of Man" to correct popular messianic expectations. At the same time he uses it to emphasize that God's Messiah must suffer on behalf "of many" (10:45; cf. 2:10). Thus, divine necessity and human opposition converge in the death of the Son of Man. Mark 10:45 contains a particularly unique reference to the suffering Son of Man: "The Son of Man has not come to be served but to serve and to give his life as a ransom for many." This is an exceptional self-identification of Jesus. It goes even deeper than Mark 8:31, because here Jesus interprets the meaning of his impending death.

Furthermore, many scholars agree that Jesus alludes here to Isaiah 53[11]; a reference "to give your life as a ransom for many" recalls Isaiah 53:8, which speaks of the one who was "stricken for the transgression of my people." The only "problem" is, in Isaiah 53 the term used is "Servant of Yahweh" (*Ebed Yahweh*), while Jesus speaks of the "Son of Man" in Mark 10:45. However, since Jesus' entire demeanor supports his identification with the Servant of Isaiah 53, it is very likely that Jesus himself establishes this connection: the Servant of Yahweh is the humble Son of Man, and, by implication, the Servant of Yahweh is thus also the exalted Son of Man of Daniel 7:13 (see the exaltation of the Servant in Isa. 53:10–12). Both Jesus' actions and his references

11. See, e.g., Oscar Cullmann, *Christology*.

to the suffering Son of Man (Mark 8:31; 10:45) point to the double theme of rejection and substitutionary suffering of the "Servant of Yahweh" (Isa. 53:8). The exalted state of the Messiah is severely buffeted by his humiliation, but it is never abolished.

Isaiah 53 is both unusual and exceptional in its context. On the surface, there is a problem with the interpretation of Isaiah 42–53. The standard Jewish interpretation of the so-called "Servant of Yahweh songs" in these chapters is that the "Servant of Yahweh" represents the people of Israel. The understanding of the persecuted people of Israel is that as the collective "Servant of Yahweh" they endure much difficulty and humiliation. In fact, many sections in Isaiah 42–52 can be interpreted in this manner; they may very well represent Israel as a suffering people. However, it is very difficult to apply this interpretation to Isaiah 52:13–53:12, because here one individual servant of Yahweh suffers on behalf of his people. If we define "Servant of Yahweh" as referring collectively to Israel, then Israel would suffer in Isaiah 52:13–53:12 on behalf of Israel, effectively atoning for itself.

There is, then, a wonderful explanation for the identity of the "Servant of Yahweh" in the context of Isaiah 42–53. The "Servant of Yahweh," which may very well be collective Israel, suffers. However, it is the royal leader of the people who will suffer and give his life as an atonement on behalf of the people (Isa. 52:13–53:12), just as Mark tells us in 10:45. The suffering people of God are purified and healed by their royal leader and head.

When Jesus begins his public ministry, he goes to the Jordan to repent, like everybody else who was drawn by the Spirit of God. While Jesus has nothing personally to repent of, he acts as an intercessor for the people of Israel, who go to the Jordan to be baptized in their repentance. He brings pure repentance to God on behalf of the people by identifying fully with them and with their lot. As Daniel prays on behalf of the sin of his people by saying, "We have sinned" (Dan. 9:5), so Jesus, being pure in heart and without sin, already begins to suffer on behalf of his people when he identifies with them in repentance.

Third, the phrase "Son of Man" is also known in an apocalyptic context, based on Daniel 7:13–14, where the exaltation and authority of a "Son of Man" before the "Ancient of Days" is emphasized.[12] It is Jesus as the honored Son of Man who forgives sins directly (Mark 2:10; a prerogative reserved for God alone), who is the Lord over the Sabbath (2:28), and who ultimately judges humankind (8:38; 13:26). In Daniel 7:13–14 (cf. Dan. 7:15ff.) the Son of Man receives worship together with the Ancient of Days and rules over the people of God together with the Ancient of Days.

Jesus, the Messiah of God, as LORD. The significant identification of "Jesus as Lord" has its origin in Jesus' own interpretation of Psalm 110:1–5. The Greek term *kyrios* (Lord) was used by pre-Christian translators of the Hebrew Bible (LXX) to render both Yahweh and Adonai. The question is, then, how this term came to be associated with Jesus of Nazareth. An initial hint might come from Mark 2:28, where Jesus states that the Son of Man is "Lord" of the Sabbath. The key text for the identification of "Jesus as Lord," however, is Mark 12:35–37. Here, Jesus identifies the messianic "son" of David as the "Lord of David" (cf. 10:47–48). Psalm 110:1 is thus taken by Jesus as a reference to himself as the Adonai (Lord) to whom Yahweh (LORD) speaks (see also Mark 14:62). The exaltation of Adonai to the right hand of Yahweh (Ps. 110:1) and subsequent subjugation of Adonai's enemies point to the following interpretation: as in Philippians 2:8–11, Jesus as Lord is exalted to coregency with God the Father and thus shares in the divine nature with the Father (cf. Phil. 2:9–11 with Isa. 45:22–23).

While Jesus establishes this crucial link between Psalm 110:1–5 and the exalted Messiah as Lord in Mark 12:35–37, he reinforces it during his trial before the high priest (14:62). The high priest's central calling is to intercede before God on behalf of Israel. When Jesus answers the high priest's question about whether he is the Messiah, the Son of the Blessed, he combines references to Daniel 7:13–14 and Psalm 110:1 in his reply. Mark 14:62

---

12. Especially in Ezekiel, the phrase "son of man" refers to the prophet.

represents a unique combination of these two passages. These are very interesting passages in that they both appear to challenge a basic tenet of the Old Testament, namely, that God will not share his glory with another (cf. Isa. 42:8; 48:11).

Surprisingly, both Daniel 7:13–14 and Psalm 110:1–5 explicitly state that Yahweh does share his glory with someone. In Daniel 7:13, God, or the Ancient of Days, shares his glory with a "Son of Man," and in Psalm 110:1, 5 Yahweh shares his glory with *Adoni/ Adonai*, the "Lord of David." In reality, these two passages allow a glimpse at the complexity of the one God. As the rose opens into three petals, we see the triune God. Only in this way do these passages, which could be interpreted by Jews in a messianic sense at the time of Jesus, make any sense in the consistently monotheistic context of the Old Testament. There is little evidence to show that a messianic hopeful around the time of Jesus claimed to be either the fulfillment of Daniel 7:13–14 or of Psalm 110:1–5.[13] Furthermore, there is virtually no evidence that a messianic figure before Jesus claimed to be the fulfillment of both. Mark 14:62 represents such an audacious combination that the high priest, as God's official representative, has full justification to accuse Jesus of blaspheming the very person of Yahweh. Either Jesus challenges the exclusive glory of the true God and must rightly be executed for blasphemy, or he is indeed a member of the one, triune, and eternal God.

The affirmation of Jesus by the heavenly Father is thus highly significant. God the Father is "pleased" in his Son (1:11), he endorses him as his "beloved Son" (9:7), glorifies him (Acts 3:13), and raises him from the dead (Acts 3:26; 1 Cor. 15:3–11). The fact of the resurrection of Jesus verifies and supports Jesus' divine claims. This means that God the Father stands behind the humiliation and exaltation of his eternal Son. Even though the Father curses Jesus by crucifixion on account of our sin, he exalts him and thus renders his death a substitutionary atonement. The trial and condemnation of Jesus only makes histori-

13. See Darrell Bock, *Blasphemy and Exaltation in Judaism: The Charge against Jesus in Mark 14:53–65* (Grand Rapids: Baker, 2000).

cal sense if indeed Jesus does make such a lofty and dangerous claim; a claim which is vindicated by his physical resurrection from death to eternal immortality.

The Connection between Jesus' Teaching on the Kingdom of God and His Self-Revelation (Mark 14:25)[14]

Now that we have a grasp of Jesus' teaching of the kingdom rule of God and of Jesus' self-disclosure as both a lowly and a highly exalted being, we may trace his own connection between kingdom rule and himself. It is significant that, prior to Mark 14:25, Jesus mostly teaches separately either about the messianic kingdom of God or the identity of God's Messiah. Until this point he does not explicitly link the coming kingdom of God with his own person as God's appointed Messiah. After Jesus has clarified in his previous teaching both the unique character of God's messianic kingdom and the identity of God's Messiah, he then provides the link in Mark 14:25.

The thematic connection between Mark 14:25 and the entire narrative of Mark shows that Jesus' demonstrated authority is connected with his future kingly rule. The death and resurrection of the Messiah mark the actual inauguration (see 14:22–24 and the "blood of the covenant") of the eternal messianic rule.

Mark 14:25 is best paraphrased as follows: "As surely as I am now not any more drinking from the fruit of the vine, so surely will I drink it again in the kingdom of God." Jesus anticipates an interim period between his death and the messianic banquet, regarding which (cf. 1QSa 2:11ff.) there is a thematic connection between "victory," "celebration," "banquet," the "presence of the Messiah," "judgment," and "pilgrimage of the nations" (see 1 Chron. 12:38–40; Isa. 25:6–8; 34:5–7; 54:5–55:5; Joel 2:24–6; Zech. 9:15; cf. Matt. 22:1–10; Mark 2:18–20; and Rev. 19:7–9). Once Mark 14:25 and 14:62 are seen together, there remains no doubt that the vindicated Son of Man (Dan. 7:13–14:22, 27), as well as

14. See also above, chapter 3, pp. 37–38.

the enthroned Lord of David (Ps. 110:1–5) rules presently over his universal kingdom (cf. Acts 2:30).

The messenger of the kingdom is simultaneously its king. While there remain many detailed questions regarding the exact character of this messianic kingdom, one thing is now certain: he who died a substitutionary death determines both the character of the kingdom and who enters it. Believers commune now with the risen Christ (e.g., in the Lord's Supper as acceptance of his atonement and as anticipation of the future messianic banquet). On account of Mark 14:25 and its context, it becomes clear that the future messianic kingdom is inseparably connected with the present rule of Christ over his people.

Conclusion

The ultimate message of Mark consists of a direct call to individual and collective discipleship under the kingly rule of Jesus in the setting of the messianic and eternal kingdom of God. The readers/hearers become aware of the fact that Jesus' deeds and teachings lead to a division between his opponents and followers. The hearers take note that the call to discipleship is encompassed by the humility and greatness of the one who calls. He leads toward a community of all who will submit to the rule of God. To do so, readers are directly confronted with the crucifixion of the powerful Messiah on their behalf (15:37; 10:45). Prior to Jesus' death, scoffers and opponents voice their views. Subsequent to the crucifixion only those who honor, confess, and believe are mentioned. Between these two types of respondents, Mark narrates the crucifixion of God's eternal Son. For a moment, time stands still as the reader faces both the cross and a profound personal challenge.

As God's Messiah, Jesus is the Son of God, the Son of Man, and Lord. As such, he displays great humility as well as power and authority. He possesses power over natural forces (e.g., 4:35ff.; 6:45ff.), demons (e.g., 1:23ff.; 3:11–12), and sickness (e.g., 1:29ff.;

2:3ff., and others). Jesus interprets the Torah authoritatively (e.g., 1:21 ff.; 2:23 ff.; 7:1 ff.; 10:1 ff.). He is the inaugurator of the eternal kingdom of God. The consequence of this reality for discipleship cannot be overstated. No less a person than God himself calls us to follow him (1:16–17; 9:2–8). The call to discipleship occurs as the triune God involves himself directly with the disciples by means of the incarnate Son of God. While Jesus appears as a mere human being, ready to suffer, he turns out to be God the Son as well. The disciples are thus not following a new teacher, but God himself. They are not involved in a human movement but in the unfolding of the kingdom and rule of God. They are captivated by God's ultimate reversal of the consequences of humankind's rebellion against its Maker.

5

Jesus' Fundamental Challenge to the Twelve and to All Disciples

I think all Christians would agree with me if I said that though Christianity seems at first to be all about morality, all about duties and rules and guilt and virtue, yet it leads you on, out of all that, into something beyond. One has a glimpse of a country where they do not talk of those things, except perhaps as a joke. Everyone there is filled full with what we should call goodness as a mirror is filled with light. But they do not call it goodness. They do not call it anything. They are not thinking of it. They are too busy looking at the source from which it comes. (C. S. Lewis)[1]

Our preceding discussion teaches us that Jesus' call to discipleship reverses the fall of man and involves a renewed dependence upon God. Jesus' arrival triggers a culminating process of God's pursuing his people and calling them to himself. Discipleship is thus a reality both in the context of creation and fall as well as in the context of redemptive-historical renewal. Jesus arises as the climactic fulfillment of God's redemptive plan that was inaugurated in Genesis 3:15. He calls his disciples into a dependent relationship which reverses the primeval fall of man away

1. C. S. Lewis, *Mere Christianity* (London: Macmillan, 1952), 149.

61

from walking with God. The ultimate antidote to such autonomy and resistance is dependence upon God's grace, based on Jesus' atonement (Mark 10:45). The call to discipleship is thus a call to reliance on Jesus for restoration of life with God rather than on autonomous human effort.

Not only is the coming of Christ a fulfillment of prophecy, but his call to discipleship represents God's culminating pursuit of his people. Discipleship, therefore, brings real hope in that it is not just a movement of following Jesus now, but marks the beginning of an eternal relationship. God's Messiah arises as the eternal King, presiding over a rule that will never end. Consequently, Jesus' call to discipleship marks the beginning of a process in which disciples will ultimately reign with the triune God (Dan. 7:15ff.).

The eternal King of the messianic kingdom establishes patterns characteristic of his kingdom by means of his own character and example. He shapes his followers according to analogous patterns (pattern-imitation). At the beginning of this transformation, Jesus acts as a catalyst of honest self-disclosure on their part. This provides deep insight into the heart of Jesus' work: to call the disciples from autonomy to dependence upon God. This call does not focus on changing behavior but rather on changing fundamental attitudes of the heart, which in turn will shape behavior.

Despite their religious upbringing, the disciples persist in self-dependence, for both their day-to-day lives as well as their understanding of God and his will. The disciples come to Jesus with fixed religious ideas, which are a selective sample from the Old Testament as taught by Pharisaic synagogue teachers during the disciples' early adolescence. Jesus does not only teach a defined "curriculum," but intends to reshape their thinking and heart-attitude toward themselves and God, thus affecting every aspect of their lives. Jesus pursues nothing less than the complete reshaping of the disciples in mind and heart. The Gospel openly describes the initial transformation which the disciples undergo under Jesus' influence.

Later, we will address the question of transferability from the initial disciples to all disciples. Here we merely note our conviction that these fundamental questions posed to the initial disciples do apply to all disciples. Christ came to those who realize, through the work of the Holy Spirit, that they are "ill" at heart (see Mark 2:17).

The Double Crisis of Self-Perception and God-Perception

Jesus begins the process of discipleship by posing two core questions to his disciples:

"Who do you perceive yourself to be?"
"Who do you perceive God to be?"

These two questions lead to a double crisis[2] in the lives of the disciples. We submit that this double crisis clears the field to lay the foundation for true discipleship as holistic dependence upon the triune God. Circumventing this double crisis leads to a false concept of discipleship, which most often deteriorates into pursuing a mere set of rules or disciplines.

As mentioned above, the central issue of discipleship operates in the larger biblical framework of God's restoration-mission throughout the ages, in anticipation of the coming kingdom of God. The double crisis into which Jesus leads his disciples is meant to open their hearts to their need for reconciliation with God and a life of dependence on God as a foundation for existence as God intended. Accordingly, the double crisis shows how the messianic rule of God begins its impact.

The biblical restoration-mission of God answers, according to Christopher Wright,[3] the four essential questions of existence:

1. Where are we? We inhabit the earth, which is part of the good creation of the one living, personal God.

2. I am using the word crisis not in the existentialist sense but in the sense of the Greek term *krinein*, which means "to decide," "to judge, following serious consideration."
3. Christopher J. H. Wright, *The Mission of God: Unlocking the Bible's Grand Narrative* (Downers Grove, IL: InterVarsity, 2006), 55, drawing on Craig Bartholomew and Michael Goheen, "Story and Biblical Theology," in *Out of Egypt: Biblical Theology and Biblical Interpretation*, ed. Craig Bartholomew, et al. (Grand Rapids: Zondervan, 2004), 144–71.

2. Who are we? We are human persons made by this God in his own image. We are creatures of this God but unique among them in spiritual and moral relationships and responsibilities.
3. What's gone wrong? Through rebellion and disobedience against our Creator God, we have generated the mess that we now see around us at every level of our lives, relationships, and environment.
4. What's the solution? Nothing in and of ourselves. But the solution has been initiated by God through his choice and creation of a people, Israel, through whom God intends eventually to bring blessing to all nations of the earth.

This restoration-mission is fulfilled—and is also in the process of being realized—in and through Christ among his worldwide people. The way Jesus begins to provide ultimate and lasting answers to these four essential questions is to challenge his disciples (then and now) to understand themselves and to face the one and only true God. Becoming—and being—followers of Christ thus takes up the center of the overall redemptive-historical purpose of God.

Part of Christ's work in the disciples and in us is to lead to an ever-deepening conviction of our persistent self-sufficient state. Jesus aims, as a consequence, to foster an ever-growing realization of our need to surrender to him and his reconciling work. Why? In order that we may live in his unmerited gracious provisions as well as to realize who the true God really is. In this way we discover on a fundamental level that this true God really loves us and that he reconciles us with himself to transform us into image bearers of Christ. In this way the triune God resolves the double crisis and develops core characteristics in each of his followers in accord with kingdom patterns, expressing God's character.

While this classic (Augustinian and Calvinist[4]) dual focus is central, we must note that the theocentric resolution of self-

4. My colleague, Jerram Barrs, drew my attention to the following quote from Calvin: "It is certain that man never achieves a clear knowledge of himself unless he has first looked upon God's face" (John Calvin, *Institutes of the Christian Religion*, trans. Ford Lewis Battles, ed. John McNeil (Philadelphia: Westminster John Knox Press, 1960), 1.1.1.).

perception (I am loved into godliness) and God-perception (God is eternally triune and includes me/us in his mission) has clear interpersonal consequences.[5] In the end, loving God with mind and heart, loving self, and loving others are interrelated realities.

Finally, all reconciled image bearers of God have particular, nontransferable personality traits which will come into full fruition. Far from becoming less of a person in Christ, each disciple develops his/her full personality and gifting.

The Crisis of Self-Perception

Mark Twain had this to say about knowing ourselves: "I think we never become really and genuinely our entire and honest selves until we are dead. And not then, until we have been dead years and years. People ought to start dead and then they would be honest so much earlier."[6]

At the forecourt of the temple of Apollo at Delphi visitors could read: "Know Thyself." The phrase is attributed to various Greek thinkers and especially to Socrates. The challenge to "know oneself" is also the subject of one of Alexander Pope's poems entitled "Essay on Man."[7] It reflects what Blaise Pascal called (in French) "the misery and the glory" of the human condition and what others described in various other terms, seeking to capture the paradox of human nature.[8]

> Know then thyself, presume not God to scan;
> The proper study of humankind is Man

5. Augsberger speaks of a "tri-polar" approach in contrast to the classic "bi-polar" view. See David Augsburger, *Dissident Discipleship: A Spirituality of Self-Surrender, Love of God and Love of Neighbor* (Brazos Press: Grand Rapids, 2006), especially the Introduction.

6. *Mark Twain's Library of Humor* (New York: Modern Library, 2000), xiii.

7. This poem was published in 1734.

8. Calvin states: "We are ruined statues in which we can still trace outlines of our former glory." Elsewhere Calvin says to "look to the image of God in them, an image which, covering and obliterating their faults, should by its beauty and dignity allure us to love and embrace them" (Calvin, *Institutes*, 3.7.6). The influential educator Parker Palmer, in *The Courage to Teach: Exploring the Inner Landscape of a Teacher's Life*, Tenth Anniversary Edition (San Francisco: Jossey-Bass, 2007), 113, passes on an apparent Hasidic tale, which says: "We need a coat with two pockets. In one pocket there is dust, and in the other pocket there is gold. We need a coat with two pockets to remind us who we are."

Placed on this isthmus of a middle state,
A being darkly wise and rudely great:
With too much knowledge for the Sceptic side,
With too much weakness for the Stoic's pride,
He hangs between; in doubt to act or rest,
In doubt to deem himself a God or Beast,
In doubt his mind or body to prefer;
Born but to die, and reasoning but to err;
Alike in ignorance, his reason such
Whether he thinks too little or too much:
Chaos of thought and passion, all confused;
Still by himself abused, or disabused;
Created half to rise and half to fall;
Great lord of all things, yet a prey to all;
Sole judge of truth, in endless error hurled:
The glory, jest, and riddle of the world!

Here the deist Pope argues contrary to Jesus' call by encouraging humans to "scan" humankind strictly by means of human resources. But Jesus argues that it is God who must "scan" us, so that we can see our true selves.[9]

Shakespeare is much more direct than Pope concerning the problem of human nature.[10]

What a piece of work is a man, how noble in reason, how infinite in faculties; in form and moving how express and admirable, in action how like an angel, in apprehension how like a god: the beauty of the world, the paragon of animals!
—*Hamlet*, Act II, Scene II, lines 300–304

I am myself indifferent honest, but yet I could accuse me of such things that it were better my mother had not borne me:

9. See, similarly, Ralph Waldo Emerson's 1831 poem "Gnothi Seauton" (which is transcribed Greek meaning "know thyself"). Emerson expressly claims that we need no external perspective. All we need is to know and "save" ourselves. First published in *The Journals and Miscellaneous Notebooks of Ralph Waldo Emerson* (Cambridge, MA: Harvard University Press, 1960–82).

10. For this reference I am indebted to my colleague and Shakespeare specialist, Prof. Jerram Barrs.

I am very proud, revengeful, ambitious, with more offenses at my beck than I have thoughts to put them in, imagination to give them shape, or time to act them in. What should such fellows as I do crawling between earth and heaven? We are arrant knaves all; believe none of us.

—*Hamlet*, Act III, Scene I, lines 123–29

Jesus challenges his disciples with similarly searching and radical questions: "Do you know who you really are? Do you know what is really in you?" We find this focus particularly in Mark 7 and 8. The question does not primarily address something like a Myers/Briggs self-assessment of temperaments and personality, as helpful as those can be. In Jesus' double question, he is not just seeking to address a person's particular DNA, habits, morals, and values. The question aims rather at our fundamental human nature in both its defaced brokenness and its reflection of original glory and God-given purpose.[11] In other words, Jesus addresses problems of the fundamental make-up of a person, problems whose solutions profoundly affect the particular personality of each human being.

Jesus approaches the question of the disciples' self-perception in four primary ways.

The Defilement of the Heart (Mark 7:14–23). While treating this passage more fully later,[12] here we mention that the various heart-defilements of Mark 7:20–23 are of such pervasive depth that their cleansing has exercised Stoics, ascetics, and earnest Pharisees alike.[13] Although Jesus does not describe here how these profound heart-defilements might be removed, he confronts his disciples with their stark reality.

11. See especially David Benner, *The Gift of Being Yourself: The Sacred Call to Self-Discovery* (Downers Grove, IL: InterVarsity, 2004), and J. Richard Middleton and Brian J. Walsh, *Truth Is Stranger Than It Used To Be: Biblical Faith in a Postmodern Age* (Downers Grove, IL: InterVarsity, 1995), 46–62.

12. See below, chapter 6, pp. 109–12.

13. See Paul's critique of Stoic, ascetic, and Pharisaic attempts at removing the defilements of the power of sin in Col. 2:23.

Jesus' Prophetic Acts of Mercy (Mark 7:31–35 and 8:22–26). Jesus healed a deaf-mute person in 7:31–35 and a blind person in 8:22–26. Both of these healings are figurative warnings regarding the disciples' proper "hearing" and "seeing" (see below, Mark 8:17–21). Jesus not only warns the disciples directly, but also engages in prophetic acts (as Isaiah, Jeremiah, and Hosea did) to underscore his words. As Jesus heals to express God's mercy, he simultaneously teaches his disciples by means of prophetic acts.

The content of Mark 8:22–26 is not found in Matthew, Luke, or John. Why does Jesus heal the blind man in two stages? We know of ancient accounts where healing a blind person was considered to be the greatest of miracles. We must ask, however, whether Jesus was capable of healing a blind person right away. Clearly, he was (Mark 10:46–52; John 9:1–41). As stated above, one of the dynamics in the first half of Mark's Gospel is that Jesus demonstrates increasing authority over various aspects of life. He has authority over demonic powers, over the laws of nature, over physical ailments, and he teaches with direct authority. It is, then, right to conclude that Jesus could have healed the blind man in Mark 8:22–26 right away.

We believe that Jesus heals the blind man in two stages to confront his disciples with their hardness of heart.[14] Jesus functions as Old Testament prophets whose words and acts instruct. Hosea, for example, was called to underline his message to Israel by marrying a prostitute, which served to illustrate the broken relationship between hard-hearted Israel and God. Likewise, Jesus teaches through prophetic acts. We observe this on the literary level because there are no less than eight words for "seeing" in these short five verses. Repetition ("blind," "eyes," "see," "looked up," "see" unclearly, "opened his eyes," "sight," "saw everything clearly") occurs for emphasis, and in this case probably

14. See Craig Blomberg, William Klein, and Robert Hubbard Jr., *Introduction to Biblical Interpretation* (Waco, TX: Word Books, 1993), who speak of finding the "natural" meaning of a text, i.e., the intended meaning—at times literal, at times both literal and figurative, and, at times, figurative.

for overemphasis, thus pointing to the disciples' figurative lack of "seeing." We suggest that Jesus heals the blind man in two stages (Mark 8:22ff.) to teach the disciples two important facts about their own hearts: (1) their inner darkness hinders their seeing themselves (it is as if Jesus says, "Do you also not see and hear?"); and (2) their blindness prevents them from seeing who Jesus really is. Though they are perhaps beginning to see who they really are and who Jesus really is (cf. 8:29), they do not see clearly yet. Seeing clearly requires much change of heart. All of this echoes the prophetic warnings in Jeremiah and Isaiah to a people with hard hearts.

Figurative "Blindness" and "Deafness" (Mark 8:17–21). Jesus says in Mark 8:17–18, "Do you not yet perceive or understand? Are your hearts hardened? Having eyes do you not see, and having ears do you not hear?" He uses the references to "hearing" and "seeing" in a metaphorical, figurative way.[15] Mark 8:17–21[16] clearly challenges the disciples to take a closer look at themselves, the lack of which also hinders them from seeing who Jesus really is.

Contrary to this warning, the disciples opine that they are in a very good place. They may even have been led to believe that they are fine, based on what Jesus said to them personally in Mark 4:10–12.[17] There, Jesus focuses on the hard hearts of those who are "outside," applying the warning of Isaiah 6:9–10 to them:

> Go, and say to this people:
> "Keep on hearing, but do not understand;
> keep on seeing, but do not perceive.
> Make the heart of this people dull,
> and their ears heavy,
> and blind their eyes;

15. See the extensive Old Testament, especially prophetic, background to the figurative use of "seeing" and "hearing." See, e.g., Isa. 6:9–10; Jer. 5:21–22; 6:10.

16. See further discussion below, pp. 109–12.

17. Note that Mark 4 uses the word "hear" 14 times; a point made by one of my students, Jon Coody.

> lest they see with their eyes,
>   and hear with their ears,
> and understand with their hearts,
>   and turn and be healed."

While this passage does probably speak of hardening for judgment, Jesus speaks in parables to those "outside" (see, e.g., Mark 12:1–12) as a severe warning, still offering the possibility of repentance (cf. 4:33–34). Now, however, Jesus warns his disciples, those on the "inside," of just that kind of hard-heartedness! It is therefore appropriate to conclude that what distinguishes the disciples from those "outside" is that they remain under the influence of Jesus to change their hearts.

Jesus' Figurative Reference to "Yeast" (Mark 8:15). "Watch out," Jesus warned them. "Beware of the leaven of the Pharisees and the leaven of Herod" (8:15). If you mentioned "leaven" or "yeast" in a figurative sense among first-century Jews, you would probably be understood as referring to Gentiles. Associating with Gentiles, those who worship other gods, and those who do not walk according to God's laws brought defilement. From the Pharisees' perspective that defilement was known as "yeast." In Jesus' usage, the "yeast of the Pharisees and of Herod [Antipas]" refers to a different kind of defilement. It denotes something that leads people to oppose the purposes of God. On the surface it is curious to see the Pharisees and Herod Antipas lumped together in one phrase. If you had asked the Pharisees what they thought of Herod Antipas, they would have declared him unclean. He was collaborating with the suppressive Roman Empire. He was corrupt in so many ways. He was living against the ways of God. But why would they, as law-abiding Pharisees, be warned of the same "yeast"?

The figurative use of "leaven" or "yeast" by Jesus generally describes a destructive pervasiveness. It is something that leads people to oppose Jesus and the ways of God. Luke 12:1 uses "yeast" figuratively in terms of "hypocrisy," 1 Corinthians 5:6–8 uses it

70

in the sense of "self-praise," and Galatians 5:9 uses it as "self-righteousness." Interestingly, later rabbinic Judaism identifies the metaphor "yeast" or "leaven" with the evil inclinations in all human beings (*yetzer ha-ra*).[18] Jesus thus says: Pharisees and Herod are pretending to be something that they are not, presenting themselves as "healthy" and whole persons, assured that they are fine with God, whole in themselves and their relationships.

The shocking fact, however, is that Jesus does not say, "Stay away from the yeast of the Pharisees and of Herod Antipas." He does not say, "Look at these people outside who are full of self-praise, hypocrisy, and self-righteousness." Rather, Jesus says, "You, my disciples, are exposed to, endangered by—yes, harboring—that same attitude" (cf. Mark 7:20–23). The disciples are thus not in a better place than Jesus' opponents. Most likely, Peter and the disciples had a "them" and "us" mentality. It is so easy to expose what is outside of ourselves.

Because of Jesus' sacrificial love, we are safe to begin a process of being completely truthful about ourselves. We are met by a capable physician who comes to us and says, "I already know." When Jesus asks the disciples questions, he is not seeking to gain information. Rather, by asking, he seeks to trigger a process of self-understanding. When Jesus asks, "Having eyes do you not see, and having ears do you not hear?" (8:18), he confronts them with themselves. He pursues the ultimate purpose of cleansing their hearts so that their inner eyes and ears would open and be amazed about two things: how sick they really are and how powerful and good Jesus really is. We are called to full honesty because the One who has the power to heal us already knows our condition. We can rest assured that we will not surprise our Master with anything he will discover in our souls. So why keep it hidden? Why live with it anymore? Why continue a divided life between the outside (pretense) and inside (reality)? Why continue

---

18. See Berachot 17a (second to third century A.D.). See Claude Montefiore and Herbert Loewe, eds., *A Rabbinic Anthology* (London: n.p., 1938), 300–01, 362, 578. See Marcus Borg, *Conflict, Holiness, and Politics in the Teachings of Jesus*, rev. ed. (Philadelphia: Trinity Press International, 1998). See also Exod. 12:15–17, where "yeast" is connected with having to rush the bread-baking process on account of imminent judgment and deliverance.

that hopeless battle when, in fact, the One who calls us has the power to overturn our self-centeredness?

Rather than understanding the call to discipleship primarily as a call to exercises and performance, we should see it, at the very heart, as surrender to the love of God. It is surrender to the liberation of truth, to the "exodus" from our own autonomy by embracing the substitutionary atonement of Christ. It is the liberation of the soul through the power of Jesus. Without that liberation, there will not be liberty and strength to live godly lives. It is the love and the kindness of God that frees us to surrender. We are not forced into being disciples of Jesus. We surrender to the One who pursues us in sacrificial love, kindness, and deep knowledge of our inner selves. We can trust God's loving pursuit of us because he does this not merely to show us the weight of our inner lives, but to liberate us from it with the cleansing assurance of his love.

The Crisis of God-Perception

> The instrument through which you see God is your whole self. And if a man's self is not kept clean and bright, his glimpse of God will be blurred. (C. S. Lewis)[19]

Jesus' call to self-exposure involves more than just a call to know ourselves. He not only confronts his disciples with the truth about their deficient perception of themselves, but also with their deficient perception of God. The second crisis is triggered by the startling question, "Who do you perceive God to be?"

To appreciate this question properly, we must gain an in-depth sense of what it meant that Jesus arose in Palestinian Judaism in the first century A.D. We must be able to empathize with the disciples' persistent lack of understanding. We must also seek to understand the anger and resistance of Jesus' opponents. We must understand why the high priest rigorously prosecuted Jesus, especially during the trial at night by the Sanhedrin. If

19. C. S. Lewis, *Mere Christianity* (London: HarperCollins, 2001 ed.), 89.

we cannot sympathize with them, we cannot develop a sense of the profound "crisis of theology" which Jesus set in motion.[20] In Jesus' presence, we are to consider who we really are in the eyes of God and, even more importantly, who God really is based on his self-revelation.

In order to find out how Jesus leads his disciples into the crisis of their God-perception, we need to recall what we observed concerning Mark's structure. Mark basically consists of two parts: the first dealing with the manifestation of Jesus' power and the second with the testing of his power and claims. From the very beginning Jesus knows the purpose for which he came. Already in Mark 2:19–20 he says, "As long as they have the bridegroom with them they cannot fast. The days will come when the bridegroom is taken away from them. . . ." The phrase "the bridegroom is taken away from them" echoes Isaiah 53:8. It already casts a dark shadow on Jesus' life. And the "shadow" is this: Jesus knows that in order to inaugurate the eternal kingdom of God among a purified people, he must undergo sacrifice and make atonement.

The crisis of the disciples' perception of God deepens, however, with the opening of the second part of Mark (8:27ff.). The transition from verse 26 to verse 27 is very dramatic. Geographically we are at the northernmost point of the ministry of Jesus in Galilee, Caesarea Philippi, which is close to the source of the Jordan River. The Jordan flows south, paving the way, so to speak, for the last journey of Jesus to Jericho and then up the wadi to Jerusalem. During this last journey, Jesus begins a rigorous training of the disciples concerning the question of who God's Messiah really is. Jesus confronts them with the fact that the Messiah is both a divine and human being who is called to die an atoning death.

When the disciples first begin to follow Jesus, their views of God, the Messiah, and humanity are all intact and settled. They know who Yahweh is; they know that the Messiah is to be

---

20. As noted above, we use "crisis" not in the existentialist sense but in the general sense of the Greek *krinein* "to decide," "to judge, following serious consideration."

the earthly Davidic King. And they know that they belong to the chosen covenant people of God and, as such, are the beneficiaries of God's blessings. But in the presence of Jesus and his teaching, all of that is shaken.

Jesus, the teacher of heart-transformation, asks a leading question to begin a process in the disciples: "Who do people say that I am?" (8:27). This question leads them to sort through the prevailing different popular views about Jesus (8:28). The disciples say, "Some people perceive you to be John the Baptist." According to Mark, even Herod Antipas held the superstition that the decapitated John the Baptist had come back and been revived in the person of Jesus (6:16: "John, whom I beheaded, has been raised"). This view is a mixture of belief in fate and the fear of punishment by a vindictive God. In retrospect, however, it is based on ignorance. Luke 1:17 is very clear that John the Baptist came "in the spirit of Elijah." John the Baptist is thus not a reincarnation of Elijah. Rather, Elijah continues to be Elijah after his death as signified in his appearance on the mount of transfiguration (Mark 9:4). There was, however, an expectation that one like Elijah would come "in the spirit of Elijah" to "prepare the way of Yahweh" (Mal. 4:5). And this, indeed, Jesus affirms after the account of the mount of transfiguration, as having occurred in the coming of John the Baptist (Mark 9:12). Finally, it is based on ignorance since the Baptist and Jesus met (1:9).

A second common perception was that Jesus is "one of the prophets." This probably refers to the prophet like Moses. Moses, the greatly respected giver of the law, points beyond himself to a coming prophet by saying: "The LORD your God will raise up for you a prophet like me from among you, from your brothers—it is to him you shall listen. . . . And I will put my words in his mouth, and he shall speak to them all that I command him. And whoever will not listen to my words that he shall speak in my name, I myself will require it of him" (Deut. 18:15, 18–19). It is indeed true that Jesus is that prophet (cf. Acts 3:22; 7:37). However, in the popular expectation of the day, this prophet would function like a political savior; as

74

did Moses, the prophet like Moses would lead the people to political liberation.

The third expectation is that Jesus is the coming Elijah who prepares the way of Yahweh. This is falsified by Jesus' own teaching, which connects Elijah with the coming of John the Baptist (Mark 9:12). Jesus is not the forerunner who comes in the "spirit of Elijah" (Luke 1:17) to call people to repentance. Rather, he is the one of whom the forerunner (John the Baptist) speaks (Mark 1:7–8).

Reviewing popular perspectives on Jesus is as important for us as it was for the first disciples. Who do we perceive the Master to be? Do we domesticate Jesus merely as the "Lord of the church," the "Lord of my personal prayers," or the "Lord of my family"? Or do we bow before him as the Lord of the universe, the Lord over political rulers and business leaders, the Lord over creation and his church, the Lord to whom we are to submit rather than merely asking him to bless what we do?

Jesus furthers this process by asking the probing question, "But who do you say that I am?" (8:29). The question forces the disciples to face their own hearts honestly. It is the indirect approach of a gentle but purposeful teacher. Jesus knows that as he proceeds to that central question he exposes the mixed perceptions of Peter's heart (spokesperson for the Twelve), as Peter in effect says both, "You are the Messiah" and "I have a preconceived plan for how your messianic life should go." Obviously, the parallel passage in Matthew 16:17 states that Jesus confirms Peter's confession of the Messiah as having been revealed by God. We are, however, dealing with a more complex issue. To realize that Jesus is the Messiah is the result of a God-given perspective on Jesus. And yet, the view Peter has of that Messiah is still very limited. When Peter says, "You are the Messiah," he implies, "you are going to sit on the throne of David in Jerusalem after having liberated Israel from Roman occupation." We can infer this from Jesus' chastisement of Peter in Mark 8:32–33. By divine revelation Peter confesses that Jesus is the Messiah, and yet, he holds to human expectations for the Messiah which directly oppose God's very purposes.

75

The Gospel of Mark describes the disciples' lack of understanding as a problem of the heart rather than an inability to understand words. Again and again we are confronted with the question of hardness of heart. Later on, Peter will preach in Jerusalem that the Jewish leaders had "the Author of life" killed, rejecting the very life-giver (Acts 3:15). This shows that hardness of heart will stop at nothing. It persists in guarding the status quo and maintaining a fixed agenda even in the face of evidence that runs counter to its expectations. That is why we can say with Paul that our intellectual perspectives are primarily driven by the disposition of our hearts, not so much by objective cognition (Col. 1:21–22). Jesus therefore "de-contextualizes" Peter's perceptions and expectations. He has to separate for Peter his culturally conditioned ideas and the truth of God with regard to Jesus' identity.

As mentioned in chapter 4, Jesus corrects Peter's messianic views by using the phrase "Son of Man," among other approaches. Jesus thus ingeniously links divergent Old Testament anticipations of God's Messiah to accomplish this correction. Now, Jesus does something even more radical to make himself and his central purpose known. As he and his disciples turn south and travel along the Jordan, he gives the first major prediction of his death and resurrection. In fact, Mark 8–10 contains three such predictions.

Every time Jesus makes this prediction, he adds an instruction on discipleship. Already Mark's literary structure tells us that what happens to Jesus will affect his disciples too. Not only do we get to know Jesus, but, simultaneously, we begin to realize who he is who imprints himself on us. Studying Jesus means coming to understand increasingly the one who shapes us and whom we will reflect in Christlike character traits. We will always remain creatures and human beings, but we will be "conformed to the image of his Son" (Rom. 8:29). We will be patterned after his character and manner of life (Rom. 12:2; 2 Cor. 3:18; Col. 3:10). The demeanor of our Master will be imprinted on our demeanor. Jesus' announcement that the Son of Man will

76

suffer has consequences for the followers. Jesus has to die to remove, once and for all, our alienation. In addition, Jesus' death will be, in an analogical way, our dying to self-determination. He will be rejected, killed, and raised after three days. The life of the follower will be marked by patterns analogous to those in the life of the Master.

Not only does Jesus speak of his suffering, but he identifies it as a divine necessity. Jesus says, "The Son of Man *must* die" (Mark 8:31, italics added). Why this urgency of his death? Peter might think: "Can't we do this differently? Can't we just teach people to renew their trust in God and give them your wisdom? Can't we go to Jerusalem and with supernatural power and the use of guerrilla warfare get a restored theocracy established in Jerusalem? Why does the hope-bearer of a restored kingdom in Jerusalem have to die? I have staked my hopes on you. If you don't work out, who will give us hope?"

Shortly after Peter's confession of Jesus as the Messiah, Jesus says, "Get behind me, Satan! For you are not setting your mind on the things of God, but on the things of man" (8:32–33). The origin of Peter's ideas is his fallenness, not God. Jesus is not identifying Peter as Satan; rather, his idea is satanic. Peter harbors an evil perspective. We have to be very careful not to demonize everything, but there is a very sobering convergence between the satanic world and our autonomy. The criticism of Peter toward Jesus arises from mere human thought. The attitude in verses 32 and 33 is one of Peter taking charge. It is very presumptuous. And Satan's purposes converge with the effort to abandon the divine necessity of Jesus' death. We note, therefore, that divine insight and truth can stand side by side with evil and self-serving perspectives. This is why we have to remain humble and teachable at all times.

It is very helpful in this context to recall the foot-washing scene recorded in John 13. Jesus has to break through to Peter in a much deeper way than Peter is prepared for. He does not realize that his refusal to see the divine necessity of Jesus' death is connected with the condition of his own heart. Jesus, the

Son of Man, has no need to die for himself; rather, the urgent necessity of his death pertains to Peter and all other followers of Christ. In the foot-washing scene, Jesus begins to kneel and wash Peter's feet. Peter thinks, "No way! This is not what you have come to do. This is not honorable for the Messiah. I am following you; you don't serve me. Remember, we have a plan together; sometimes I have to help you remember who you are. You are my Master, and I am serving you, so sit down and let me wash your feet." In contrast, Jesus challenges Peter to the very core of his being. "If you want to have any part in me, I must wash your feet." The Son of Man has not come to be served but to serve and to give his life for the sanguine Peter, the devious tax collector Matthew, the political activist Judas, the meditative John, and you and me. Jesus has to break through the barrier of the hard heart and set ways of Peter and us all.

It can be dangerous merely to *know about* Jesus' atonement. Therefore, it is necessary that we go through a process of "letting Jesus wash our feet." We have to realize that Jesus breaks open our hearts with the power of his love, going deeper than may be comfortable for us. Once Jesus gains our heart through his love, we will have to be his. The ultimate problem of Peter is not the role reversal of master and servant. The ultimate problem is one of control and Peter's blindness to his own self-sufficiency and his wounds. Peter must surrender his plan for Jesus' life and accept Jesus' plan for his life. In Jesus' love we lose the self-sufficiency (the "yeast" of the Pharisees and Herod), which Jesus exposes in the original disciples and in us. C. S. Lewis once said:

> To love at all is to be vulnerable. Love anything, and your heart will certainly be wrung and possibly broken. If you want to make sure of keeping it intact, you must give your heart to no one, not even to an animal. Wrap it carefully round with hobbies and little luxuries; avoid all entanglements; lock it up safe in the casket or coffin of your selfishness. But in that

78

casket—safe, dark, motionless, airless—it will change. It will not be broken; it will become unbreakable, impenetrable, irredeemable.[21]

The danger of knowing about Jesus' atonement in a merely cognitive way is that it does not impact the deepest core of one's being.

Paul will later say in Romans 8:32: "He who did not spare his own Son but gave him up for us all, how will he not also with him graciously give us all things?" The fundamental issue of conversion is surrender. If God has loved us by giving us his Son, will he not give us all things necessary for our growth in him? The promise is conditioned on his will and his provision. The motivating force for Jesus' substitutionary death is profound love that upholds justice. I have to rely on the work of the Spirit of God in my own heart for God's love to break through. What John testifies to, I have to let sink in: "For God loved the world so much that he even gave his only begotten Son that whoever would put trust in him would enjoy an eternal relationship with the triune God and not perish in separation from God" (John 3:16, paraphrased). To say in my culture, "God loves me," sounds rather romantic and unrealistic. It is the hardest thing for me to accept. In fact, I wonder if the root of much ungodliness in our lives, the root of our idols, the root of our adulterous thoughts and actions, the root of our addictions, the root of our pride, the root of our rebellion against God, is the fundamental resistance to the true love of the eternal Son of God for us.

Let us ask the living triune God to give us a heart receptive to his love. "We love because he first loved us" (1 John 4:19). We must surrender to the pursuit of God in our lives. Are our affections focused on God or on some other person or object? Is the love of God so substantial that nothing in this life will be able to shake it? May the love of God be like a radiant sunrise in the morning which softens us into willing surrender, opening our eyes to his care.

21. C. S. Lewis, *The Four Loves* (New York: Harcourt, 1960), 21.

The Interrelationship of the Two Crises, Their Resolution, and Tri-Polar Effect[22]

The Interrelationship of the Two Crises

> To see God as God is—not as who we want God to be— requires that we see our self as we actually are. For the same cloud of illusions obscures our view of both God and ourselves. (David Benner)[23]

Unless we enter the crisis of self-perception, we will not see our dire need for the justifying and healing atonement of the incarnate Son of God. Unless we enter into the crisis of our God-perception (Mark 8:31–33), we will not see the depth of who God really is and the rescue and healing that he brings to us. Jesus' call to discipleship leads to both a radical self-assessment and a radical review of who we perceive God to be. We are dealing with an interrelated dynamic, a double, reciprocal crisis that revolutionizes life in all its facets. A radical assessment is necessary in which God's self-disclosure through his eternal Son (the crisis of God-perception) becomes the surprising answer to the crisis of self-perception. Without God pursuing us, we cannot truly know ourselves.

An instructive biblical example for knowing ourselves only in the light of God's self-revelation is the conversion of Paul. When Paul, then known as Saul, went to Damascus he was full of zeal for Palestinian Judaism as he had learned it. He was very sure that he was seeking to execute Christians because they were blaspheming heretics. In his own mind, he was serving God with his whole heart, being one of the best educated teachers of the law of his time, and being more zealous for the God of Israel than many of his colleagues.

22. David Augsburger, *Dissident Discipleship: A Spirituality of Self-Surrender, Love of God, and Love of Neighbor* (Grand Rapids: Brazos Books, 2006), speaks of a tri-polar foundation of discipleship: a reconciled relationship with God, self, and others. While we uphold the dual nature of Jesus' central challenge to his disciples ("do you know yourselves?" and "do you know God?"), Augsburger correctly draws attention to the tri-polar effect of the resolution of the double crisis of reconciliation, which includes relationship to others.

23. Benner, *The Gift of Being Yourself*, 63.

As he goes to Damascus he hears a voice from heaven. Saul, at this moment, finds himself in the midst of the crisis of self-perception and God-perception because he has to realize that this Jesus who speaks to him is loved by God the Father, whom Saul supposedly worships. In Saul's conversion, the God of the Old Testament becomes more complex. The Father that he worships says, "I love my Son. You cannot have me without the Son" (Acts 3:13).

This encounter with the risen Christ also shows Saul who he really is. Paul's subsequent teaching on the severity of human-kind's alienation from and enmity toward God stems from this encounter with the risen Christ. Christ does not say, "Saul, please believe that I am the Messiah. You are doing fairly well already. You are a good teacher. Please, just add one more thing for my sake: I want to be known as your Messiah." Christ does not say, "Your understanding of some laws of the Old Testament is not quite right. You need to make a few adjustments." The conversion of Saul is not a minor modification of the status quo. Rather, Paul confesses later that he was shown to be an enemy of God (Rom. 5:10; 1 Cor. 15:9). As he encounters the risen Christ, Saul sees, for the first time, who he really is in the light of God's glorious presence. Saul had to move from a man-centered religiosity to a thorough dependence on God.

Without the knowledge of God we will not have a true knowledge of self, and without the knowledge of self we will not have a full knowledge of God. There is a reciprocity which is initiated by God's revelation. The two questions of self-perception and God-perception are intertwined. We cannot give the answer to one without affecting the other. Discipleship, then, is not essentially a matter of how we should conduct ourselves. It is not chiefly a matter of moral decision, but it is more fundamentally a matter of Christ's exposure—and transformation—of our self-perception and God-perception.

The Resolution of the Double Crisis and Its Tri-Polar Effect

Three relational dimensions are affected by our alienation from God: our relationship with God himself, our relationship with ourselves, and our relationships with others. The double crisis which Jesus provokes touches our very identity as human beings in these three areas. Fundamental identity questions seem very impractical and, at times, frustratingly elusive. Nevertheless, they still frame and shape our every thought and action. You may test yourself by reflecting on the following two statements. Someone says to you: "You are lovable"; someone else says: "You are useless." The effect that each statement has on your fundamental perception of yourself has a tremendous impact on every area of your identity and life.

The Resolution to the Crisis of a Man-centered Self-Perception. If we do not see ourselves as Christ sees us—as self-sufficient and broken as well as exceedingly loved and precious to God—we will be disciples who miss Jesus' core call. He calls us to repent in an ongoing way from our autonomy and to turn to ever-increasing dependence on him in the midst of his ongoing love in all areas of our lives. If we do not learn to see ourselves as Christ sees us, we will merely "do" Christianity without radical, sustained inner change. That is exactly the plight of the orthodox Pharisees at the time of Jesus, who are so close to—and yet so far from—God's purposes.

While Jesus does give specific ethical instructions to his disciples, these instructions rest on the above-mentioned fundamental questions regarding the true knowledge of God and the true knowledge of self and others. When that realization has sunk in, then and only then, may we ask, "How would you have me to live, Lord?" "What is abhorrent before your righteous throne?"

The Resolution to the Crisis of a Man-centered God-Perception. If we do not see our true selves, we will be disciples who do not really need the Jesus of the Gospels. All we really need is a wise teacher of some aphorisms. If we do not see our true selves, we will not enter into the crisis of our God-perception to accept the necessity of the incarnation of the eternal Son of God for our rescue. We must ask ourselves: do we really sense the dire need for Jesus' rescue or do we merely render lip-service to his call and work?

The Communal Effect of the God-centered Resolution to the Double Crisis. If we do not recognize our true selves and God's deep, triune self-revelation through Christ, we will not be free to grow in loving others. We will not be captivated by Christ's communal kingdom purpose with a sober self-assessment and a corporate reflection of Jesus' patterns of humility (see Mark 9:31 for context and 10:35–45). We must let Christ captivate all of our affections, cultivating an ever-growing, sober view of ourselves, so that we might love our neighbor as ourselves.

Unless we are healed by God's view of ourselves through his self-revelation, we will remain mostly autonomous, unchanged people. We will be correct in our confession of faith but personally stagnant and essentially alone. The discovery of our real self as we understand Christ's love-pursuit leads us toward embracing Christ's communal purpose. This is true because much of Jesus' teaching on discipleship in Mark 9 and 10 involves his followers' being shaped by him in the midst of a Christ-minded community.[24]

The ever-deepening double crisis of self-perception and God-perception shapes our understanding of our reconciliation with God through Christ's atonement. It also deepens our healing and facilitates our participation in a new humanity. It is significant to note, therefore, that Jesus speaks of the coming tribulation (Mark 13)[25] as a corporate experience. Jesus combines a radical realism about who we really are with a profound, covenantal, unparalleled pursuit of us in love. And this leads us toward the identity, demeanor, and behavior of his new community. While we need to be transformed individually, there is always a communal effect.

A further consequence of the communal effect of discipleship is that growth in discipleship involves reciprocal elements.[26] Even

---

24. See, e.g., Mark 3:33–35 and 10:35–45 in their respective contexts: there is a serving community.
25. See the accumulation of plural pronouns.
26. See chapters 7 and 8 of this book.

the call to "make disciples" in Matthew 28:19–20 is based on the humility of progressively becoming disciples of Christ ourselves. What is the result? The effect of Christ's redemptive work in the life of the disciple leads to God-given communal relationships which, in turn, lead to reciprocal growth in maturity (see Eph. 4:1–16).

Implications for All Disciples: The Disciple as a "Saved Sinner"

We have quietly assumed a fundamental transferability of these core issues raised by Jesus from the initial disciples to all followers. In the introduction to this chapter we have, however, already noted that Jesus came to heal the sick and unrighteous (Mark 2:17). Any persons, then, who realize such heart-sickness, when quickened by the Holy Spirit, may embrace Jesus' teaching and atonement (10:45, "for many") for their healing and transformation. What Jesus chisels into the hearts of the initial disciples, he thus intends for every disciple. We will see this truth reinforced when we discuss Jesus' general call to discipleship in Mark 8:34.[27]

For some students of the New Testament, however, it is not clear that every person, saved by Christ's completed work, still needs to grow in godliness so that the reality established by Christ becomes reality in daily life. This process is sometimes referred to as progressive sanctification. These students claim that, following conversion, every aspect of the old life is passé. According to them, no struggle should be found in the life of a true follower of Christ, no sign of sin, no weakness.

Contrary to that view and in accord with the Reformers' stress on the Christian's life as *simul iustus et peccator* ("at the same time justified and a sinner"), we stress that every aspect of discipleship discussed in this book is part of such progressive sanctification following conversion. Both the double crisis of self-perception and God-perception, as well as the eight core characteristics of disciples (see chapters 5–7) must be subsumed

27. See below, pp. 99–105 and Appendix B.

under the category of progressive sanctification. For the unconvinced, we submit for consideration the following sampling of the New Testament's focus on progressive sanctification of true disciples of Christ.

- The Lord's Prayer (Matt. 6:9–13), which is given for disciples' continued dedication to God, emphasizes that forgiveness of sins (both from God and toward others) is an ongoing process, although always based on Jesus' finished work.
- In the parable of the sower (Mark 4:1–9, 13–20), Jesus not only speaks about unbelievers' hearts, but also indicates that fruit-bearing comes in time to believers by God's grace. He also teaches that perhaps such fruit-bearing will even overcome some of the hindrances (opposition/temptations) mentioned in the first part of the parable.
- John admonishes Christ's disciples to confess their sins (1 John 1:8–10; 2:1; see also John 8:7; Rom. 14:23) and thus to be dedicated to the truth. They are to walk continuously in the light and life of Jesus (John 8:12; 15:1–8).
- Paul would not have needed to write his epistles if the true followers of Christ[28] were perfected at the point of conversion. The very issues that Paul has to address drive home the fact that while the recipients of his letters were set apart ("saints") and secure in the grace of God through Christ's atonement, they nevertheless struggled with great sin. He writes of confusion, strife, rivalry, pride, self-righteousness, greed, sexual promiscuity and impurity, etc. Paul addresses his readers as both justified and sanctified in Christ (e.g., 1 Cor. 1:2; Rom 1:7; 8:1, 28–39), while speaking of all manner of sins to be overcome in their progressive sanctification or ongoing discipleship. Not only does Paul speak about many moral struggles,

28. While Paul does not use the terminology "disciple," there are many thematic connections between discipleship patterns in the Gospels and Christian growth patterns in Paul's Epistles. See Stephan Smallman, *The Walk: Steps for New and Renewed Followers of Jesus* (Phillipsburg, NJ: P&R Publishing, 2009).

but he also speaks as himself having undergone purification and much suffering as a disciple of Christ (2 Cor. 6:1–10). Toward the end of his life, Paul calls himself "the foremost" of sinners (1 Tim. 1:15).

- Each disciple is admonished to continue being conformed to the image of him who saved him (Col. 3:10). This implies that the transformation from autonomy and self-centeredness to proper perceptions of self and God toward true worship and godliness is an ongoing process.

- This process of the disciple's purification is also emphasized in Paul's and Peter's repeated reference to ongoing "dying" and "rising" with Christ (e.g., Rom. 6:1–23; Col. 2:11–14; 1 Peter 2:24). Similarly, Paul addresses true followers of Christ with the admonition to "put to death the flesh" (Rom. 8:13; Gal. 5:19; Col. 3:1, 5), which means letting go of self-centered ways of thinking, being, and acting. In addition, Paul admonishes the believers and disciples to live godly lives (Rom. 13:13–14), which means to think and act in a God-dependent way. Paul stresses that whatever is not of faith is sin (Rom. 14:23b), implying that a disciple can still think and act in a "faithless" (i.e., sinful) state.

- James admonishes Christ's disciples to confess their sins to each other (James 5:14–16). The writer to the Hebrews identifies Jesus as the High Priest who makes intercession for his people (Heb. 4:14–16). Why would he do so, if not for their weakness and sin? Moreover, we are exhorted to flee from sin (Heb. 11:25; 12:1, 4; James 1:15).

- The revelations of John, containing various messages to churches in Asia Minor, address groups of disciples. The exalted Christ calls the true believers in Ephesus (Rev. 2:5) to repent and to return to their first love, Christ, and thus to the triune God. Jesus searches the hearts of the believers in Pergamum (Rev. 2:23). If they were already completely pure, why would Jesus warn them? Why would Jesus discipline the disciples in Laodicea, whom he loves, if they were completely free from sin (Rev. 3:17–19)?

Conclusion

We have sought to show that the essential element of Jesus' call to discipleship is his confronting his disciples with two fundamentally unsettling questions: "Who do you perceive yourself to be?" and "Who do you perceive God to be?"

This double question leads to a fundamental double crisis in the disciples' lives. From Jesus' perspective, his disciples neither know who they are in God's eyes, nor who God really is. Once the disciples begin to face this double crisis, they enter the field of true discipleship which leads to a holistic dependence upon the triune God. They gradually realize that their state of sinful self-sufficiency is much more severe in God's eyes than they had assumed ("they dress the wound of my people as though it were not serious," Jer. 6:14; 8:11; NIV). They also begin to realize that the God they thought they knew differs from their new understanding of him. In fact, he is triune and as such graciously heals their profound alienation through the atonement of the eternal Son. Jesus not only serves as the catalyst of their double crisis, but also leads them to its resolution by restoring them to eternal dependence upon the true triune God of the universe. Jesus resolves this double crisis by restoring his followers to the triune God and by overwhelming them with a deep sense of his atoning and healing love despite their rebellious alienation. At the same time he also lays the groundwork for restoring relationships among human beings and restoring their relationship to the rest of creation.

In the light of these considerations, we must emphasize that if a follower of Christ would want to avoid this double crisis, he or she would miss the fundamental reckoning with self-perception and God-perception. Such avoidance would put the dire need for Christ's atonement in danger of being marginalized. Discipleship would be in danger of degenerating to the mere pursuit of a set of rules or disciplines.

6

Christlike Character

WE HAVE SEEN that true followers of Christ cannot avoid facing the double question that fundamentally challenges everything on which they base their lives: "Who do you perceive yourself to be?" and "Who do you perceive God to be?" One consequence of Jesus' double question is that each of his followers has to accept his or her inability to mend the broken relationship with the Creator and its effect on human relationships. This broken relationship is at the heart of God's self-revelation in Scripture and lies at the center of the double crisis.

Indeed, the paradox of life is best explained by this revelation: On the one hand, creation (including human beings) reflects traces of great beauty, meaning, and complexity. On the other hand, it is filled with destructive and defacing ugliness and death. The biblical answer to this paradox is that while God created all things in goodness and wholeness, the willful rebellion of humankind into mental and moral autonomy has permeated all areas of life with brokenness, ugliness, and destruction (cf. Rom. 8:19–23). The brokenness is so fundamental and has reached such proportions that only God himself can redress it.

Jesus' coming provides reconciliation and restoration with God, thus answering both fundamental questions. Because of reconciliation with God we can know who God really is. Consequently, we can also know who we really are in the eyes of God. Jesus' coming is not the coming of a mere religious leader or some new god, but rather the coming of a member of the eternal Trinity. Jesus is the Son who is sent by the Father and equipped by the Holy Spirit. The Father identifies himself so closely with Jesus (Mark 1:11; 9:7; Acts 3:13, 15; John 17:5, 24) that to deny one is to deny the other.

Surrendering to the atoning healing of Jesus (Isa. 53:5) and thereby finding reconciliation with God (Mark 10:45; Rom. 3:21–26) leads to entry into the rule of God (Mark 4:20; 10:15). Acceptance of Jesus' leadership means affirming the order of creation. Entry into the kingdom of God is reentry into the creation order by restorative forgiveness.

The rule of God stands above political structures, national affiliations, and ethnic loyalties. It provides the fundamental parameters of a disciple's identity and belonging. Belonging to Jesus is belonging to his kingdom rule. Jesus' authority, will, and character form and shape the hearts and lives of his people, resulting in a God-centered worldview in contrast to rival worldviews.

Identifying Jesus' Core Characteristics for All Disciples

The eternal Son of God's fundamental answer to the double crisis of self-perception and God-perception is given in his atoning death. As a result, the disciples are now shaped individually and corporately toward a new character that reflects Christ. We thus speak of discipleship as a move toward Christlikeness.

Christ-centered, spiritual character formation affects, above all, core attitudes and behaviors. On the basis of his atoning answer to the double crisis of existence Jesus serves as example, teacher, and enabler of the character formation of all disciples. In these ways Jesus invests himself in his disciples. Eventually, all of his disciples will reflect him in his character. This expansive individual and corporate movement characterizes much of what the kingdom of God is all about.

As a core kingdom principle we note that there is a powerful ripple effect of the King's finished work, character, and behavior. On account of the profound master-follower connection, Christ exemplifies, teaches, and engenders core characteristics of godly

90

character in all disciples (except for Judas, John 17:12). This phenomenon is explicitly stated and exemplified in John 13 and implicitly described in Mark's narrative. Thus, "being conformed to Christ," "imitating Christ," and "sharing in union with Christ" are all results of the same cause: Jesus enables and facilitates the accomplishment of what he teaches, calls for, and exemplifies.

Building on the foundation of Jesus' dual challenge regarding our view of ourselves and of God, Mark conveys a cluster of core values, attitudes, and behaviors which Jesus exemplifies and makes possible in the original disciples and in us. Certainly, these are also to be sought in ourselves and others as part of our spiritual character formation.

Before we examine these eight characteristics that apply to all disciples, it is important to note that there are some elements of discipleship which are unique to the original disciples and apostles of Christ. Clearly unique to the Twelve are:

1. Their callings as apostles, which set them apart from other early followers of Christ. The unique aspects of this calling are seen in Mark 3:14 (see also Acts 1:21–22).
2. Their being sent out in Israel two by two to preach, cast out demons, and heal while under a set of restrictive travel stipulations (see Mark 6:7, 12).

The Twelve, then, are assigned unique and unparalleled functions. There is no indication in Mark that these aspects of the apostles' calling also pertain to future followers of Christ. Underlying these unique aspects, however, are some transferable principles that do indeed apply to all disciples, tying them together in a common mission. Chief among these principles are:

1. The object of our faith and allegiance is the King, who calls us into general surrender and willingness to serve. He is the same yesterday, today, and forever (Heb. 13:8). The triune God will not change. As we are called to serve him we can be assured that he will not change.

91

2. Certain core attitudes and Christlike behaviors are meant to grow in all followers of Christ.

Let us now turn to a preliminary discussion of these core attitudes (we will examine each of them in more detail in the next chapter).

The Eight Core Characteristics of Christlikeness for All Disciples

By using the criteria outlined below, we have been able to isolate eight specific core attitudes and behaviors that are fundamental to the development of Christlike disciples.

The respective characteristic has to be explicitly stated as applying to Jesus, the twelve disciples, and all disciples. For the category which applies to all disciples, we look especially for general statements in Mark beginning with such formulations as "whoever," "anyone," "everyone," and "whosoever." Among other functions, these statements often serve as introductions to general statements of discipleship.[1]

Less specific and less direct statements pertaining to all disciples supplement this list: Mark 2:17 (call to sinners); 7:28–29 (faith); 9:23 (all things are possible with God); 10:14 (let the children come to me); 10:23–27 (it is difficult for a rich person to enter the kingdom of God); 11:17 (prayer); 13:33 (be watchful).

Comparing the above references in Mark with those found in the Gospels of Matthew, Luke, and John (using the same criterion presented above),[2] reveals confirmations and reinforcements of these findings. In addition to the evidence in Mark concerning Jesus' general discipleship characteristics, Luke adds that everyone is welcome (cf. Matt. 7:8; Luke 6:47; 11:10), as well as the sharing of goods or renounc-

---

1. The ESV (supplemented by KJV and NIV) references are as follows (the most relevant ones for our topic are given in italics): "Whoever": *3:29, 35*; *7:10*; *8:35, 38*; *9:37, 41ff.*; *10:11, 15, 43–44*; *11:23*; [*16:16*]. "Anyone": 1:44; *4:23*; 7:24; *8:34*; 9:8, 30, *35*; 11:3, 16, *25*; 13:21; 16:8. "Everyone": 1:37; 5:20; *9:49*. "There is no one . . . who will not": 10:29–30. The KJV adds 6:11 "whosoever" (in addition to ESV "whoever"/"anyone" occurrences). The NIV reads "whoever" (in addition to ESV) in *4:25*; *9:40*.

2. ESV: "whoever" in the other Gospels: Matt. 5:19, 21–22, 31–32; 10:33, 37ff., 42; 12:30, 32, 50; 15:4; 16:25; 18:4ff.; 19:9; 20:26–27; 23:12, 20ff.; Luke 3:11; 9:24, 26, 48; 11:23; 14:27; 17:33; 18:17; John 3:15–16, 18, 21, 33, 36; 4:14; 5:23–24; 6:35, 37, 47, 54, 56ff.; 7:38; 8:12, 47; 11:25; 12:25, 44ff.; 13:20; 14:9, 12, 21, 24; 15:5, 23; 16:2.

ing everything at one's disposal (Luke 14:33), and finding contentment in what one has (vs. coveting). Matthew adds particular details
regarding moral aspects of the Mosaic law (including murder, insult,
adultery, coveting, and mercy). Matthew 12:30 reinforces Mark's
theme of being "with" Jesus. John strongly reinforces obedient faith
and trust in Jesus, "doing the truth," and receiving Jesus' testimony.

These findings do not necessarily indicate that there are merely
eight core attitudes and behaviors engendered in all of Jesus' disciples. It does mean, however, that these eight items are particularly
featured and emphasized in Mark. We thus do well to begin with
these eight core attitudes and behaviors as we seek to understand
Jesus' focus on character formation and the essential renewal of
redeemed humanity. More attitudes, behaviors, and exercises may
be added, based on additional aspects of Jesus' teaching.

Regarding the general statements on discipleship in Mark
we can thus speak of a "triple effect," a wave moving from Jesus
to his original disciples to all other followers of Christ. This wave
gives rise, focus, and emphasis to the following core attitudes,
which we identify as Christ-facilitated imperatives arising from
Jesus' finished work, example, and teaching. Even though Jesus
is not physically present now, the promise of the Holy Spirit's
presence (the baptism in the Holy Spirit is promised to all, Mark
1:8; cf. 1:10)[3] for all followers of Christ ensures ongoing, Christ-
engendered tutelage for growth in spiritual character formation.
The Holy Spirit, in conformity to Scripture, is the means by which
Christ's holistic character formation takes place in his disciples.

The eight core attitudes and behaviors before God, toward
ourselves, and others which we are to cultivate as disciples are:[4]

1. Surrendering (unconditionally): 14:36 (J); 10:28 (d); 10:29–30 (a);
12:44 (a); at times: money 10:21 [23–27] (a); denying yourself: 14:36
(J); 8:34–35 (d + a); bearing your cross: 14:36 (J); 8:34 (d + a), and

3. This is not a "second blessing." Rather, receiving the Holy Spirit runs concurrent
with belief in the finished work of Christ.
4. Square brackets indicate less specific and less direct statements. The (J) refers to
these characteristics as applying to Jesus, (d) refers to them as applying to the original
disciples, and (a) as applying to all disciples.

following: (being at Jesus' disposal) 1:17 (d); 2:14 (d); 4:23, 25 (a); 8:34 (a); 10:11 (a); thus doing God's will: 3:35 (d + a; including the fulfillment of God's law, avoiding legalism and antinomianism).[5]

2. *Believing and trusting*: 14:32–36 (J); [neg. 4:40 (d)]; 10:27 (d); 11:22 (d); 13:11 (d); 16:6 (d); 1:15 (d + a); [2:5 (a)]; [5:34 (a)]; [neg. 6:6 (a)]; 7:28–29 (a); 9:19, [24] (a); 11:23–24 (a); see 16:16 (d + a).

3. *Praying*: 1:35 (J); 6:46 (J); 14:32–36 (J); 9:29 (d + a?); 11:[17], 24–25 (a).

4. *Watching over—and guarding—your heart (so as to beware of hard-heartedness and lack of understanding)*: 8:33 (J); 14:36 (J); 8:17–21 (d + a?); 14:38 (d + a?); [neg. 6:52 (d)]; 3:29 (a); 4:1–20 (a); 7:14–23 (a); 9:42–47 (a).[6] Seeking the purification of the heart: 10:35–44 (d); 9:49 (a).[7]

5. *Being humble*: 10:45 (J); 14:36 (J); 10:13–16 (d); 10:42–44 (d + a); 10:15 (a); [neg. 12:38–40 (a)]; being teachable: [8:4–7 (d)]; [2:17a], and expressing a servant's heart: 9:35 (d + a?); especially when holding authority: 10:45 (J); 14:36 (J); 10:42–44 (d + a).

6. *Forgiving*: 2:5 (J); 10:45 (J); 14:36 (J); 11:25 (d + a, in the context of prayer and worship).

7. *Withstanding temptation*: 1:12–13 (J); 14:32–41 (J); 14:38 (d); withstanding persecution: 2:1–10 (J); 3:6 (J); 13:9ff. (d + a?); 13:33 (d + a?); 10:30, 37 (a); cf. 14:8 (J); 14:32–41, 53ff. (J).

8. *Confessing Christ to all humanity*: 14:36 (J; Jesus "confessed" the Father); 8:38 (d + a); preaching/proclaiming: 1:14–15, 38–39 (J); 2:2 (J); 3:14–15 (d); 13:10 (a).

5. See also John 6:38 (J).
6. See Prov. 4:23, 24–27. The Psalms encourage us to "talk to ourselves" (e.g., Pss. 42:6, 12 and 43:5).
7. See Heb. 5:7. True holiness springing from the baptism of every believer in the "Holy Spirit-and-fire" (Mark 1:8; Luke 3:16; Rom. 8:9) is based on Jesus' atonement.

What follows is a graphic presentation of the preceding section, demonstrating especially the "triple effect" from Jesus to the Twelve to all disciples as mentioned above.[8] We offer a graphic overview of the core content of character formation as a consequence of confession of sin and repentance (1:5, 14–15). While each of the eight core characteristics is connected with our relationship to God, ourselves, and others, the first three focus primarily on our relationship to God (cf. 12:30; love of God), while the remaining five focus primarily on our relationship to ourselves and to others (cf. 12:31; love of neighbor and self). See fig. 7.1.

Surprisingly, we find an aspect of each of these eight core attitudes and behaviors, in essence, in Mark 14:36 (Jesus' profoundest hour of testing) and, to a lesser degree, in Mark 10:45 (Jesus' prediction of his substitutionary atonement). The core attitudes and behaviors are the outcome of Jesus' work: his substitutionary atonement, his example, and teaching, answering the two core questions of existence.

These core attitudes and behaviors give rise to further godly attitudes and behaviors. However, for the Gospel of Mark, the principal application of these additional factors to all disciples can, at times, only be implied. Among these are the following:

1. Derivative spiritual practices, especially celebrating the Sabbath day of rest (2:23) and fasting (2:18 [9:29]).
2. Derivative deeds, especially teaching (1:21; 2:13; 6:6, 34; 9:31; 10:1); being "fishers of men" (1:17); eating with sinners (2:15); engaging in exorcism (1:23, 34; 3:11, 15; 5:1ff.); engaging in healing (1:29, 34, 42; 2:11; 3:5, 10; 5:21ff.; 6:56; 7:31ff.; 8:22ff.; 10:46ff.); and considering the messianic fellowship as the ultimate family (3:34; 10:29ff.; cf. Luke 14:26).
3. Specific sins to be overcome, especially dishonoring of parents (Mark 7:10) (a); blasphemy (3:29) (a) [cf. Luke 12:10]; being a stumbling block to the weak (Mark 9:42) (d); divorce (10:2, 17ff.) (a); not paying taxes (12:17); and pursuing the law of Moses by means of autonomous legalism or rejecting it.

8. Note: Scripture references in the table are only samples.

Fig. 7.1. Eight core characteristics of discipleship in Mark

Topic	Jesus as: Example → → → Teacher/ Facilitator→ Enabler → → →	The Twelve → → → → → → → → →	All disciples → → → → → → → → →
1. Following; Surrendering obedience; Doing God's will	14:36; see John 6:38	1:17; 2:14; 3:35; 8:34–35; 10:28	3:35; 8:34–35; 10:29–30 [2:44; 4:23, 25; 10:11, 21, 23–27]
2. Believing; Being faithful; Trusting*	14:32–36	1:15; 4:40 (neg.) 10:27; 11:22; 13:11; 16:6 [16:16]	1:15; 11:23–24; 9:19 (neg.) [2:5; 5:34; 6:6 (neg.); 7:28–29; 9:24; 16:16]
3. Praying	1:35; 6:46; 14:32–36	9:29	11:[23]24–25 [11:17] [9:29?]
4. Watching over your heart; Seeking purification	8:33; 14:36 [Heb. 7:5]	8:17–21; 10:35–44; 14:38; (neg.) 6:52	3:29; 4:1–9[10–20]; 7:14–23; 9:42–47, 49 [7:10] [14:38?]
5. Serving humbly; Being teachable	10:45; 14:36	9:33, 35, 37, 41; 10:13–16, 42–44 [8:4–7]	9:37, 41; 10:15; 10:42–44 [2:17; (neg.) 12:38–40]
6. Forgiving	2:5; 10:45; 14:36	11:25	11:[23–24], 25
7. Withstanding temptation and persecution; Being watchful	1:12–13; 2:1–10; 3:6; 14:8, 32–41 (cf. 8:31; 9:31; 10:32–34)	10:30; 13:9ff.; 13:33; 14:30, 37–38, 66–72	10:[29], 30 13:37 [13:9ff.; 13:33]
8. Confessing Christ to all; Proclaiming	J. "confesses" the Father: 1:14–15, 38–39; 2:2; 14:36	3:14–15; 8:38 [14:68]	8:38; 13:10 [9:40]

* This is strongly reinforced in John's Gospel.

We have seriously considered whether exorcism and healing (listed above, under 2) should belong to the list of eight. However, on the basis of the Markan text, it remains unclear whether the call to exorcise and to heal applies not only to the Twelve but principally also to all disciples. The issue thus becomes a broader biblical theological question pertaining to the entire New Testament and lies beyond the confines of Mark.

The following attitudes, behaviors, and spiritual exercises are especially noticeable in Jesus and his original disciples. They further complement and develop the eight core characteristics mentioned above as well as the areas mentioned under items 1–3 in the previous paragraph:

1. Being blessed by angels, Mark 1:13
2. Celebrating feasts, 14:14
3. Singing hymns, 14:26
4. Experiencing God-forsakenness, 15:34
5. Bearing fruit, 11:12, 17 (prayer)
6. Experiencing blessing, 10:29–31
7. Helping the poor, 14:7
8. Storing up treasures in heaven, 10:21, and showing caution with possessions, 10:23–27
9. Frankness/openness, 4:21
10. Generosity in judging others, 4:25
11. Simplicity, 6:8f.
12. Healthy use of respite, 6:31ff.

Conclusion

In this chapter, we asked a simple question: what are the central elements of discipleship which are explicitly binding for all disciples? Above all, we discovered that Jesus is far more interested in transforming the character of his disciples than in their particular behaviors. Jesus knows that changed hearts and minds will lead to godly actions. The eight core characteristics of surrender, trust, prayer, watchfulness over our hearts, humble service, forgiveness, withstanding temptation and persecution, and bold witness form the nucleus of Jesus' explicit call to all disciples in Mark. Other characteristics and actions supplement this core to form a full spectrum of what it means to be a follower of Christ. Let us now turn to a more detailed study of each of the eight core characteristics of discipleship.

Eight Discipleship Qualities

1. Surrender to God's Will

Following: Mark 1:17; 2:14; 3:35; 5:37; 8:34–38; 10:21, 28–30; 12:44; [14:13]

(Surrendered) obedience: [1:27: demons]; [4:41: wind]; 4:23, 25; 10:11

Doing God's will: 3:35

Focus text: Mark 8:34–37: The cost and goal of discipleship.

Concept Description

This involves cutting all ties and dependencies (including idols and addictions) that inhibit our full availability to Christ and thus obedience to God's will. It means surrendering control of self-determination. The result is a real-life dependence upon Christ, including love of God, love of others, and love of self (Mark 12:30–31).

JESUS: Jesus surrendered fully to the Father and obeyed his will (14:36; see John 6:38).

ALL: Based on Jesus' ability to work the fruit of surrender and obedience in our hearts, we should ask the following questions:

1. To what extent am I surrendering to God?[1] To what extent am I obeying God?

1. These formulations arose with the help of my wife, Susan, and my colleague Dr. Donald Guthrie during a team-taught class entitled Teaching Discipleship in Mark at Covenant Theological Seminary, St. Louis, during the fall semesters of 2009 and 2010.

2. To what extent does this affect my relationship with others and myself?
3. To what extent do I teach and convey 1 and 2 above to others?

Introduction

Jesus' initial call of his disciples (Mark 1:17; 2:14) includes at least two elements. First, he calls them to "be with him" (3:14) as well as to follow him (see below on 8:34–38). Second, he calls them to learn to become "fishers of men."

"Following Christ" initially means to "leave behind and to go along with Christ" (1:17; 2:14; 5:37; see also 10:28–30; 14:13). In the broader sense it means "to let go of all that which hinders full availability and service to Christ" (see as examples 4:23, 25; 10:11, 21; 12:44), to appropriate Christ's provisions and example in communion with him, and to follow his instructions (e.g., 8:34–38). Since Christ comes in the name of the Father (14:36; 13:32), following Jesus means doing the "will of God" (3:35).

Becoming "fishers of men." Arising from this communion with and shaping by Christ is the call to become "fishers of men." The image is connected with Jeremiah 16:14–21. The context of the core verse (Jer. 16:16) speaks of God's judgment in the form of the Babylonian exile (Jer. 16:14–15). Following this punishment, God says, in the context of cleansing, that he will send messengers to "fish" his people back (to himself). The figurative use of "fishing," then, refers to the gracious restoration and purification (see Jer. 16:19; rejection of idols) of God's people following judgment.

In an analogous way to Jeremiah 16:14–21, God's judgment of his Son in his substitutionary death is followed by the "fishing of men" to restoration with him, again in the context of cleansing. As disciples who are both justified and in the process of being purified, Jesus' followers are called by him to point others in word and deed to restoration and purification on the basis of his work.

Detailed Comments on Mark 8:34-37

Mark 8:34–37 stands at the beginning of the second half of Mark, following Peter's confession of Jesus and the first prediction of Jesus' death and resurrection (8:31). While Jesus repeats his prediction (9:31; 10:32–34), the disciples do not understand its deeper meaning because there is more involved in knowing than merely listening to words. Jesus' repeated statements of the necessity of his death are like a pregnant woman's repeated contractions prior to giving birth. As such, Jesus points to his impending crisis in Jerusalem. The second prediction of Jesus' death and resurrection (9:31) is relatively brief. If you translate its core back from Greek into Aramaic, it is: *"bar anash bene anashim,"* "Son of Man into the hands of men." Even if people have no idea what *"bar anash bene anashim"* means, many will still remember its sound. As a wordplay (paronomasia) it embeds itself into the memory. After the crucifixion of Jesus, the disciples will remember "Son of Man (given for me) into the hands of men" (combining 9:31 with 10:45).

The literary structure of Mark is particularly conspicuous when each prediction of Jesus' passion (8:31; 9:31; 10:32–34) is followed by an instruction on discipleship (8:32–38; 9:33–37; 10:35–45). The very structure of this section in Mark tells us that there is an interconnection between what befalls Jesus and what happens to his disciples. He imprints his patterns on them and us. As you become a disciple of the Master, characteristics of the Master will be imprinted on your way of thinking, your way of relating, and your heart. We are essentially created to reflect God. When others look at our lives, they should see an aspect of God. When others see our relationships, they should see something of Christ. God in his mercy is carving these patterns into our lives. We are all on a journey to be transformed into the image of Christ.

Mark 8:34–38 opens the call to discipleship to all who would follow Christ (8:34). What we have said so far readily applies to followers today because Jesus continues his work through the Holy Spirit (Acts 2:33). And this is unparalleled by any other person in history. The exalted Christ operates in the visible, known world by means of the universally present Spirit of God, as much as he is reigning with the Father in the invisible, transcendent world (heaven). As we reflect on this passage regarding surrender and following God's will, we study what God intends to work into our lives. Mark 8:34 serves as the heading for the following three verses, and its meaning has often been misunderstood.

Doubtless, the classical text of the cost of discipleship is this single verse (8:34): "If anyone would come after me, let him deny himself and take up his cross and follow me." A wrong understanding of the verse would be: "If someone wants to follow me, he must deliberately deny and chastise himself; she must deliberately carry the cross of self-abasing suffering and follow me." This wrong understanding goes in the direction of egocentric self-chastisement and plays perfectly into a psychological disposition of self-abasement. According to this false interpretation any joy, any hope, must be killed. Since you are now a disciple, life must be miserable. This wrong approach leads to toiling in misery until Christ returns. It assumes a life marked only by pain and suffering.[2]

However, even a cursory study of God's people in Scripture shows that this understanding is faulty. As people like Abraham, Sarah, David, Moses, the Twelve, Mary, Paul, Phoebe, Priscilla, Aquila, Silas, Timothy, and Titus put their trust in God, follow his ways, and receive his mercy, they do not become less human. Rather, they develop and flourish. The effect of our alienation from God is, fundamentally, depersonalizing. It negatively affects the way we perceive and relate to ourselves and others. C. S. Lewis aptly observes: "When he [God] talks of their losing their selves, he means only abandoning the clamour of self-will; once they have done that, he really gives them back all their personality, and boasts (I am afraid, sincerely) that when they are wholly his they will be more themselves than ever."[3] The work of God in and through Christ to pursue us in love restores us to wholeness and personhood. Salvation means, among many other things, restoration to the image of God.

2. While pain and suffering are indeed part of discipleship, our lives must be based on dependence on God (living by the Spirit), not self-determination (living by the flesh).
3. C. S. Lewis, *The Screwtape Letters* (London: Geoffrey Bles, 1942), 59.

While all human beings still live in some respects as image bearers of God despite this alienation, the ugly effects of the fall discolor every aspect of human existence. The restoration through Christ liberates us to live individually and corporately as true image bearers of God. This means that we are people who are again becoming whole—emotionally, intellectually, and physically. By God's grace we glorify God in all we do. Christ's disciples are not diminished in personhood and significance, but are instead restored to true existence.

The very coming of the eternal Son of God to the disciples and to us means that we are valuable in God's eyes (see Matt. 6:26; 10:31; 12:12; Luke 12:7, 24). Christ's death for us speaks of his love for us and of the value he attributes to our humble lives and the grand goal of godliness to God's honor. Some of us suffer from a negative self-image. Maybe as children we had been told that we were not important. Maybe we were not encouraged. Or maybe we just have this voice inside of us saying, "I am no good." Rather than a call to self-abasement, Mark 8:34 summons us essentially to the surrender of control. This includes surrendering to God the self-abasing inner voice as a form of "negative pride." You are not meant to calculate your worth, even by self-abasement. Instead, you will now have to say to yourself: "The eternal God loves me, and he seals that love by the sacrificial death of his eternal Son. Who am I to say that I am no good if God attributes such significance to me?"

There is, then, a fundamental flaw in the above-mentioned wrong interpretation of Mark 8:34. The problem is this: in self-abasement self is still in control and remains at the center of our being. If following Christ is, at its heart, transferring control to him and letting him be at the center of your life, how can you still retain control in order to self-abase? With this wrong interpretation, you are "self-denying" by making yourself small. You yourself wrongly define what it means to "bear the cross," namely, to go through the hardship and martyrdom of life in self-centered self-reliance.

Given these concerns, a more text-based paraphrase of the passage in question would be: "If anyone would wish to follow me on an ongoing basis, let him surrender all self-sufficiency to me, live a sacrificial life as pardoned by my crucifixion, and continually follow me into true life." There is thus a clear goal in Mark 8:34: the aim is not self-denial; the aim is not "carrying the cross," but rather being at the free disposal of Jesus. How, we may ask, can you follow Christ after having turned yourself into nothing? How can you really follow Christ if you continue to take charge of your self-abasing self-denial? How is it possible to receive the love of Christ if you persist in man-centered, miserable self-management which the Bible calls "sin" and Paul calls "flesh"? We have to move away from such a misinterpretation of this verse.

The goal of discipleship is to be fully redeemed, transformed, and living as radiant letters to others of God's unmerited mercy and healing. We have to see the tough challenges of "self-denial" and "carrying one's cross" not as goals in themselves but as means to the goal—being freed to follow Christ. The glorious goal is to be free for Christ's will, adventure, and ways. It is to be fully at his disposal to reflect the glory of God in our purified lives. The goal is not to be self-centered and self-abasing ("living by the flesh") but to be God-centered and God-dependent ("living by the Spirit"). This means affirming the primacy of God and his Spirit and the goodness of his physical creation. Following the will of God is not like following the will of human beings, because God's will includes his supreme knowledge of who we are and his utter goodness. The entire purpose of Mark 8:34 is to ready us for Christ-dependent pattern-imitation in all of life.

We can say, therefore, that the core cost of discipleship in Mark 8:34 is the surrender of self-generated, self-determined life.[4] In this sense, Dietrich Bonhoeffer's[5] emphasis on "death" as the "cost of discipleship" is correct. This is true as long as we realize that "death" stands for a radical surrender, a giving over of self-centered perspectives and control to God. This might, in some cases, also lead to physical death, but in all cases it constitutes a complete loss of

---

4. Augustine (see his *Confessions*, A.D. 397–98) and Thomas à Kempis (see his *Imitation of Christ*, 1418) rightly focus on surrender to God. But both have too negative a view of the value of the physical world (especially Thomas à Kempis), which is to be enjoyed so long as a person lives in dependence upon God and seeks to worship God in all areas of life.
5. Dietrich Bonhoeffer, *The Cost of Discipleship* (New York: Macmillan, 1966).

self-sufficiency and self-centeredness. We must note, however, that Jesus never called for death without also giving life. He said: "Truly, truly, I say to you, unless a grain of wheat falls into the earth and dies, it remains alone; but if it dies, it bears much fruit" (John 12:24).

Some of us focus on "death" only. We may be tempted to be self-centered in our self-mortification. But the goal of the call to discipleship is life in Christ-dependence. This results in a community of people who are being purified, who are not afraid to be in various settings of contemporary culture because the power and claim of the Master is stronger than the claim of the culture.

It is very important to understand that the cost of discipleship includes love for the individual personality that God created, including our own. According to Leviticus 19:18, we are called to love our neighbor as we love ourselves (Mark 12:31). In this sense we differ both with Bonhoeffer[6] and Karl Barth[7] who both appear to advocate the forgetting of ourselves in order to see Christ only. While the Christ-centered focus is foundational and central, redemption affirms God's creation of the individual personality by transforming it. It is decidedly focused on God, while transforming that which God created (i.e., the personality and individuality of each person). The resurrection of Christ and that of every human being serves as the paradigm for this reality.

2. Faith in God

Believing: 1:15; 5:36; 9:19, 24, 42; 10:27; 11:23–24, 31; 13:11, 21; 15:32; 16:6, [11, 13, 16, 17]

Having faith: 2:5; 4:40; 5:34; 10:52; 11:22

Focus text: Mark 11:22–24, 31: Faith in God who "moves mountains."[8]

6. See our reflections on Mark 8:34 and Bonhoeffer's *The Cost of Discipleship* in appendix B.

7. See Karl Barth, "The Call to Discipleship" in *Church Dogmatics* 4:2: *The Doctrine of Reconciliation*, Part 2 (London: T&T Clark, 1967), paragraph 66, "The Sanctification of Man," 533–53.

8. For details on Mark 11:22–25, see section 3 below.

Concept Description

This involves conforming trustingly and prayerfully to God's purpose and putting our weight on his will as we turn away from rebellion and self-centeredness. It means counting on Jesus' (and with him, the entire Godhead's) power to work his will into our lives. It is growing in persistent confidence in Jesus' presence and help as opposed to insisting on a principal denial of trust or maintaining a skeptical distance (= deadly doubt). This involves consciously entrusting ourselves to Jesus in the midst of unbelief (9:24). Deadly doubt must thus be distinguished from constructive doubt. In constructive doubt we humbly wrestle with the challenge of being able to trust Jesus wholeheartedly. In deadly doubt we persist in a skeptical posture toward God. Trust and fear cannot coexist in our hearts (4:40; cf. 6:50).

JESUS: Jesus demonstrates ongoing dependence upon and trust in God, his Father (14:32–36).

ALL: Based on Jesus' ability to work the fruit of faith, that he both exemplifies and teaches, in our hearts, we should ask the following questions:

1. To what extent am I trusting God?
2. To what extent does point 1 remain a reality as I relate to others and myself?
3. To what extent do I teach and convey points 1 and 2 to others?

Jesus reinforces what John the Baptist had already proclaimed (1:4), namely, that the people of Israel (and thus humankind) do not start from a neutral state of heart. Rather, they find themselves in serious alienation from God which requires God-given repentance (see Lam. 5:20–21) as a prerequisite for renewed trust in God. Only the necessity of Christ's crucifixion for reconciliation discloses the full depth and severity of this alienation. In the end, only repentance and appropriating the substitutionary atonement of Christ are the means by which to redress this alienation from God.

106

Jesus teaches that faith's greatest enemy is fear (Mark 4:40; 5:36). Trust in the living and powerful God fends off the temptation to become intimidated and overwhelmed by darkness and opposition (13:11; 16:6). Weakness in faith, namely, a correctable and constructive form of doubt (9:24; [16:11, 13]), does not stand in direct antithesis to faith. Rather, growth in faith (decrease of doubt) can be addressed by petition (9:24).

The difference between faith in God and credulity must be clearly seen (13:21). Faith is neither based on complete, unequivocal proofs (15:32) nor on fiction. Instead, it is based on credible witness to Jesus (16:1–8; [16:14]). Ultimate and sustained resistance to God's self-revelation in Christ (persistent unbelief) is very serious (9:19; [16:16]) and undercuts salvation. The essence of faith is to put personal, childlike weight on God's existence, presence, and will (2:5; 5:34; 9:42; 10:52; cf. 10:27).

Prayer and trust (see section 3 below) are closely intertwined (11:24). Trust as the opposite of self-sufficiency[9] reflects an ever-growing assurance in God's will, purposes, and mission. In Mark 11:22–24 faith in God's purposes leads to the removal of idols among human beings and the restoration of true worship.

3. Prayer

Praying: 1:35; 6:46; 9:29; 11:25; 13:18; 14:32–36, 38
Focus text: Mark 11:25: The close connection between prayer and forgiveness.

Concept Description

This involves our learning to agree with, conform to, and surrender to God's purposes. It means putting our declared will consciously under God's will. Prayer includes watchfulness, resistance to the subtle temptation to follow self, joyful solitude with God, and worship of God (11:17). It is also a key tool in exorcism (9:29). Prayer

---

9. Claiming God's promises in a self-determined fashion is spiritually and emotionally dangerous.

is intimately intertwined with trust (#2), surrender to God's will (#1), and forgiveness of others (#6). The connections between prayer and fasting (as a sign of particular availability to God) may also be present.

JESUS: Jesus seeks intimate, prayerful fellowship with his heavenly Father (1:35; 6:46; 14:32–36).

ALL: Based on Jesus' ability to work the fruit of exemplified and taught prayer in our hearts, we should ask the following questions:

1. To what extent am I praying to God?
2. To what extent does point 1 remain a reality as I relate to others and myself?
3. To what extent do I teach and convey points 1 and 2 to others?

Prayer is the natural form of communion with God. By his example, Jesus draws his disciples into the same attitude and conduct of prayer. If Jesus, the Son of God, seeks communion with his Father, then we, too, need to—and are invited to—seek such communion with God as foundational to our lives. Through the Holy Spirit our eyes are gradually opened to our fundamental and ongoing need for God's presence, wisdom, and strength.

In Mark 11:22–25, three of our eight central attitudes, namely, faith (#2), prayer (#3), and forgiveness (see #6 below), are interconnected. The context of this section concerning the cursing of the fig tree and the cleansing of the temple points to one central aim: Jesus calls God's people to true and universal worship and prayer (see 11:17). As the son of the owner of the vineyard (= Israel, Isa. 5:1–7), Jesus is rightfully seeking the fruit of worship (see Mark 12:1–12). He illustrates this by means of the harsh, figurative, and representative treatment of the fig tree (11:12–14). Faith that moves mountains (a phrase clearly intended to be understood figuratively) is faith that willingly conforms to God's stated mission in contrast to our own wishes. We are thus called by God to pray confidently toward the divine removal of everything that hinders true worship (without ever treating each other disrespectfully). This most bold prayer for removal of all idolatry begins, not surprisingly, with ourselves (11:25). It involves the call to let the unmerited grace of God affect our identity in redemptive character change. This means there will be a heartfelt readiness to pass God's forgiveness on to others.

On yet another level, prayer is dedication and appeal to God that he will manifest his unparalleled power over evil (9:29).

4. Watching Over the Heart

Watching over your heart: 3:5, 29; 4:1–20; 6:50; [neg. 6:52]; 7:6, 10, 14–23

Seeking purification: 8:15, 17–21, 33; 9:42–47, 49; 10:5, 35–44; 11:23; 12:30, 33; 14:36; [16:14]

Focus texts: Mark 4:1–20: hospitable and inhospitable types of human hearts; Mark 7:14–23

Concept Description

While focusing on Christ and being receptive to his purposes, this involves keeping a vigilant eye on the condition of your heart. This means constantly returning to surrender (#1), trust (#2), and prayer (#3). Jesus lays the foundation for watching over our hearts in his fundamental challenge of the disciples and us (see above, the "crisis of self-perception," Mark 8:15, 17–21). As we continue to follow Christ, we must find out where there are elements of a hard, autonomous heart-attitude (8:17–21; 6:52) which persists in self-reliance and self-righteousness. We do not know the depths of our inner self (10:35–44). We must know increasingly what "comes out of your heart" (7:14–23). This means being radical in steering away from sin and temptation (8:33; 9:43–47). It is absolutely necessary to be purified (9:49). This means watching out for deadly doubt (11:23; see #2 above). If we are not careful, we may mislead others (9:42). Instead we must know our specific personality weaknesses and particular temptations of the heart (4:13–20). As concrete examples, this means watching over our attitudes toward our parents (7:10) and watching out for blasphemy (3:29).

109

JESUS: Jesus maintains a pure heart in the midst of all temptation (8:33; 14:36; see Heb. 7:5).

ALL: Based on Jesus' ability to produce the fruit of exemplified and taught watching over our hearts, we should ask the following questions:

1. To what extent am I watchful over my heart in relationship with God?
2. To what extent does point 1 remain a reality as I watch over my heart in relating to others and myself?
3. To what extent do I teach and convey points 1 and 2 to others?

While this fourth character trait is initially more elusive than the others, Jesus clearly leads his disciples in the direction of watchfulness over their hearts, since all attitudes and behaviors arise from the core of a person (Mark 7:6, 14–23). Jesus spends much time in confronting and acquainting his disciples with this important truth (Mark 7–8; cf. Luke 21:34–36). The entire beginning section of chapter 5 of this book is devoted to the issue of the "crisis of self-perception." Without a proper self-understanding, growth in Christlike attitudes and demeanor is impossible.

It is in this context that Mark 8:17–21 is crucial in confronting the disciples with their true hearts before God. They are exposed in their fundamental self-sufficiency, namely, hard hearts (6:50–52; 10:35–44; [16:14]), not unlike those of Jesus' opponents (see 3:5, 29; 9:42–49; 10:5).

The parable of the sower (4:1–20) provides the disciples a mirror of their hearts: will they be hospitable to Jesus' word and thus to Jesus as the Word? Will they invite the fruit of Jesus' work?

The disciples are to watch out that their prayerful hearts are free from sustained doubt (11:23). They are to "watch and pray"; i.e., to guard their hearts in prayer so they can endure temptation (14:38; see below, #7).

Jesus leads his disciples and us to face the true defilement of the core of our personhood (7:20–22). He confronts us with the fact that we do not have in and of ourselves the power and resources to reverse the defilement of our core being. Only the divine Son of God can atone for the guilt of our defilement, cleanse that defilement, and progressively heal the illnesses it carries. In the following, we give details of the various defilements mentioned by Jesus in Mark 7:20–22 with a subsequent list of reversals of these defilements initiated and facilitated by Christ.[10]

Defilements

1. Evil thoughts in general.

2. a. Sexual immorality in general (*porneia*)
   b. Theft
   c. Murder
   d. Adultery
   e. Coveting/lust for more (including sexual lust)
   f. Evil/wickedness/rejoicing in darkness

3. a. Deception
   b. Sensual greed
   c. Envy (having an "evil eye")
   d. Evil thoughts of others/slander of others
   e. Pride
   f. Foolishness/unreasonableness/unwillingness to learn

Reversals[11]

1. Thoughts aligned with God's perspective, goodness, and purpose; having the mind of Christ (Phil. 4:8)

2. a. Intergender reverence and appreciation without exploitation
   b. Reverence for/affirming/cherishing the possessions of others (physical or otherwise)

10. I am following the 1+6+6 ordering of the heart defilements listed in Mark 7:20–22 as found in William L. Lane, *The Gospel According to Mark: The English Text with Introduction, Expositions, and Notes* (Grand Rapids: Eerdmans, 1974), ad loc.

11. Some of the following formulations arose from small-group discussions (with Phil Boydell, Rhona Hastings, Roo Miller, Carmela Batluck, and James Minto) at a discipleship conference in Arbroath, Scotland, June 8, 2010.

   c. Reverence for—and nourishing—the sanctity of life

   d. Gratitude in marriage (satisfied contentment) and faithfulness of heart; communal blessing

   e. Gratitude and generosity in all of life (contentment); godly desires

   f. Rejoicing in—and nourishing—what is good, true, and honorable; friendliness; shunning evil in any form; mercy; honorable conduct

3. a. Transparent, honest life

   b. Moderation and contentment; healed affections and needs

   c. Rejoicing in possessions and success of others; looking at others as God looks at them; generosity in thought of others

   d. Speaking well of others

   e. Readiness to admit weakness and faults; deflecting attention to God and others; admitting need for God

   f. Seeking wisdom for life; being teachable and willing to grow

These Christ-driven reversals aim at the restoration of the heart toward true worship. They involve nothing less than turning from idolatrous human-centeredness to God-dependence and Christlikeness. This includes the fulfillment of the moral core of the law (Mark 12:30–31, 33; Rom. 8:4; Phil. 1:9–11) and watchful growth in godliness (see 1 Tim. 4:7b, 16).

5. Humility and Service[12]

Serve humbly: Mark 1:31; 10:45
Be teachable: 9:35, 37, 41; 10:13–16, 42–44; [neg. 12:38–40]
Focus texts: Mark 9:33–41; 10:42–44

12. C. S. Lewis, pithy as always, comments, "A man is never so proud as when striking an attitude of humility" (*Christian Reflections* [Grand Rapids: Eerdmans, 1995], 14), and "Humility, after the first shock, is a cheerful virtue" (*The Problem of Pain* [New York: HarperCollins, 2001], 62).

Concept Description

This involves serving others (cf. 9:35 and 1:31) as Christ serves us (10:45). When welcoming a person who seems to be unimportant (e.g., children in the ancient world) into our presence, we welcome Jesus and with him God the Father (9:37). Serving someone who belongs to Christ is particularly emphasized (9:41). If we are—or aspire to become—leaders or are already important in the eyes of others, we must become a servant and slave of all (10:4–44), just like Jesus (10:45). As leaders, we must not be heavy-handed, oppressive, exploitative (10:42), or ostentatious (12:38–40). Since coming under the rule of God happens by way of childlike simplicity, humility will always be a characteristic mark of kingdom life (see the life of that kingdom's ruler).

JESUS: Jesus exemplifies the greatest extremes of humility and service by dying a God-cursed, substitutionary death (10:45; 14:36). His healings are, among other things, acts of service (see, e.g., 1:31).

ALL: Based on Jesus' ability to work the fruit of exemplified and taught humility and service in our hearts, we should ask the following questions:

1. To what extent am I humbly serving God?
2. To what extent does point 1 remain a reality as I humbly serve in human relationships?
3. To what extent do I teach and convey points 1 and 2 to others?

Immediately following Jesus' second prediction of his death and resurrection (9:31), the disciples discuss among themselves "who was the greatest" (9:34). A similar scenario arises after the third prediction of Jesus' death and resurrection (10:32–34), when James and John request places of honor in Jesus' messianic rule (10:35–37). In both cases, Jesus turns the situation into a teaching moment by paradoxically inverting the human attitude and cultural approach to greatness: "If anyone would be first, he must be last of all and servant of all" (9:35; see also 10:42; 12:38–40; as well as 1:31). We find a similar statement in 10:43–44: "But whoever would be great among you must be your servant, and whoever would be first among you must be slave of all."

The statement in Mark 10:45 concerning Jesus' substitutionary atonement is the most climactic expression advocating service, humility, and sacrifice. This verse forms a sort of inclusion ("bookends") with the third prediction of Jesus' death and resurrection (10:32–34), in the midst of which is found the audacious ambition of James and John to be "great" (10:35–44).

The child whom Jesus calls to himself (9:37; see also 10:16) serves as an example of childlike humility (see also 9:41). The attitude of simple and pure humility is further illustrated in 10:13–16, where Jesus does not say that we are to become children (falsely interpreting 10:14 without looking at 10:15), but rather that we are to become childlike in our attitude to the things of God (10:15). This humble approach is conditional to entry into the kingdom of God (repentance, 1:14–15) and serves as a characteristic trait in that kingdom.

6. Forgiveness

> Forgive: 2:7, 10; 11:25 (twice)
> Forgiveness: 1:4; 3:29
> *Focus text*: Mark 11:25

Concept Description

Our forgiving others their offenses and sins is intimately connected with our coming into the presence of God in prayer (11:25a). A believer and follower of Christ who has received forgiving atonement for sins (10:45; cf. 2:7, 10; 14:23–24; cf. Rom. 3:20–26; Col. 1:21–22) is urgently exhorted to forgive others (cf. Mark 11:25). If he does not, he is met with a real but not realized[13] warning concerning God's withheld forgiveness (11:25; cf. Matt. 18:35). Repentance and forgiveness (Mark 1:4) are connected. Due to the atone-

---

13. This occurs on account of the Holy Spirit's softening a disciple's heart.

ment of Christ (10:45; 14:22–24), repentance is not the cause of or reason for our forgiveness but rather a condition of our receiving unmerited forgiveness. Since the Holy Spirit leads to repentance and conveys salvation in Christ, damning the Holy Spirit rejects God's chosen means of bringing salvation and forgiveness (3:29).

JESUS: Jesus freely forgives (2:5; including the accusations of his adversaries, 2:5–10) by giving his life as a substitutionary atonement (10:45; 14:36). Early on in Jesus' public ministry, he begins to address the theme of the removal of sin. Jesus identifies himself with the people of Israel (1:9), thus affirming that the call to repentance issued by John the Baptist is indeed from God. Simultaneously, Jesus signals his call to atone for his people. Jesus then claims the unparalleled authority to forgive sins directly, that is, as only God can forgive sins (2:7, 10). He himself pays the price of substitutionary atonement that ratifies lasting forgiveness with God (10:45; 14:36; 15:25, 37). Based on this, Jesus baptizes with the Holy Spirit (1:8; Acts 2:33).

ALL: Based on Jesus' ability to work the fruit of exemplified and taught forgiveness in our hearts, we should ask the following questions:

1. To what extent do I accept the fact that I am forgiven by God?
2. To what extent does point 1 remain a reality as I relate forgivingly to others and myself?
3. To what extent do I teach and convey points 1 and 2 to others?

Surprisingly, John the Baptist calls the people of Israel, who are privileged to have the patriarchs, adoption, the covenants, the law, the temple, and the promises (cf. Rom. 9:4–5), to repent in order that they may receive forgiveness of sins (Mark 1:4). By what means this forgiveness is attained, however, remains undefined, until the one arises to whom the Baptist points (1:7–8;

115

Rom. 9:5). He who will baptize each disciple with the Holy Spirit (Mark 1:8) will provide cleansing from sin as the condition for receiving the pure Holy Spirit. Those who blaspheme against the Holy Spirit, however, cannot be forgiven (3:29), since they resist the very agent who makes the forgiving atonement of Christ efficient. Providing forgiveness for alienation from God for human beings in their entirety is thus the unique privilege of Jesus.

We have already noted that faith/trust, prayer, and forgiveness are intimately connected in Mark (see 11:22–25). Those who confidently pray for the removal of everything that resists the true worship of God must begin with their own hearts. And they must especially begin with the very challenging issue of forgiving those who wronged them. Having received unmerited, divine forgiveness by means of the substitutionary atonement of Jesus, each disciple is to pass this on to those who have wronged him or her (see as parallel to this: "we love because he first loved us," 1 John 4:19). If this new reality, which was set in motion by God's sovereign act and grace, does not grow in the disciple, God himself will withhold forgiveness (Matt. 18:21–35). Ultimately, however, God will cause the disciple to come to repentance and willing surrender to God's forgiveness-causing power.

7. Withstanding Temptation

> Withstanding persecution: 4:17 [negatively]; 10:30
> Withstanding temptation: 14:38
> Being watchful: 13:9–13, 33–37; 14:34, 37–38
> *Focus texts*: Mark 10:30; 13:9–13, 33–37

Concept Description

This seventh core characteristic of discipleship is closely associated with #4 above. While watchfulness in #4 is directed toward the inside (8:15) of the followers, watchfulness is now

116

directed toward the outside (temptation and persecution, as well as the second coming of Christ).

This involves being watchful that we are increasingly hospitable to Christ, his word, and his purpose (4:14) so that his ways take deep roots of conviction in us (negatively in 4:17). Some form of persecution is to be expected as we follow Jesus (4:17; 10:30; 13:9–13; 14:34?). Watchfulness applies also to coming temptations and trials, in which we will be enticed to deny our dependence upon Christ. Here we must be vigilant and pray in temptation and testing (14:38). Alertness also pertains to the second coming of Christ (13:33–37). We must conduct ourselves in the light of the nearness and suddenness of his coming to final consummation and judgment. This future reality should order our priorities in our current life and assist us in living out surrender and obedience (see #1 above).

JESUS: Jesus withstands temptation and persecution (1:12–13; 2:1–10; 3:6; 14:8, 32–41). Both Satanic and human forces are opposed to his mission. Ultimately, both are rendered powerless.

ALL: Based on Jesus' ability to engender the fruit of exemplified and taught withstanding temptation and watchfulness in us, we should ask the following questions:

1. To what extent am I withstanding temptation and being watchful before God?
2. To what extent does point 1 remain a reality as I withstand temptation and am being watchful in human relationships?
3. To what extent do I teach and convey points 1 and 2 to others?

The disciple will progressively surrender to God to such a degree that external opposition, persecution (10:30), and temptation will not easily shake him or her (contrast with 4:17).

A key to this growth is to know and realize that Jesus explicitly spoke about it (13:9, 10–13). Growth in this area is further facilitated by watching and praying (14:34, 37–38), whereby our relationship of trust in the triune God increases and matures.

The disciple is to be watchful for persecution (13:9–13) and for the signs of the culmination of the end times (13:33, 37). Clearly, this points to the fact that spiritual battles are part of the disciple's reality. Both the Satanic world and human forces opposed to the ongoing rule of God will seek to obstruct dedicated and consistent service to God. Prayer is the only means by which to navigate these obstacles. Jesus is our victor; we have no strength, wisdom, or strategy apart from him.

8. Confessing Christ

Confessing Christ to all; not denying: 8:38; 14:30, 31, 72
Proclaiming: 5:20; 13:10; [16:15]
Focus texts: Mark 8:38; 13:10

Concept Description

Our relationship with Christ is crucial; it determines eternal life with—or without—God. Being ashamed of Christ before the watching world (8:38) is commensurate with persistent and ongoing denial in word and deed (cf. Matt. 16:27).[14] A natural consequence of being impacted by Christ's loving pursuit of us is that we will speak to others about him (Mark 5:20). This conforms to Christ's explicit will that "the gospel must . . . be proclaimed to all nations" (13:10; cf. 1:17; 16:15).

JESUS: Jesus confesses the Father (1:14–15, 38–39; 2:2; 14:36).

ALL: Based on Jesus' ability to work the fruit of exemplified and taught confessing and proclaiming Christ in our hearts, we should ask the following questions:

---

14. Peter denied Christ, although under life-threatening circumstances (14:30, 72). He did not persist in denial but repented deeply (14:72) and Jesus restored him (John 21:15–19).

1. To what extent am I confessing Christ in the presence of God?
2. To what extent does point 1 remain a reality as I relate to other human beings?
3. To what extent do I teach and convey points 1 and 2 to others?

Jesus came to proclaim the eternal messianic rule (kingdom) of God (1:14–15, 38; 4:1; 6:2, 34; 8:31; 12:14) and inaugurated that rule by his substitutionary atonement (10:45; 14:25). The followers of Christ are not only learners and do not only reflect essential character traits of the messianic kingdom (#1–7 above). They are also called to testify to that reality as an expression of their ongoing dependence upon Jesus (3:14; 5:20). This testimony is so intimately connected with dependence upon Jesus that eternal ramifications are associated with it (8:38; John 5:27). While eternal salvation is provided solely on the basis of the substitutionary atonement of Jesus (10:45), public confession of that reality is a necessary (and natural) outgrowth of it. But this does not mean that individual cases of denying Christ forfeit salvation (see, e.g., Peter's denial of Jesus in 14:30, 31, 72).

The public proclamation is intended for the entire world. Mark 13:10 speaks of "all nations,"[15] corresponding to the universal nature of the kingdom of God and the universal sufficiency[16] of Jesus' substitutionary atonement. This clearly implies that Jesus not only intended for his disciples to be with him, to depend upon him, and to reflect basic kingdom character traits and become Christlike. But he also intended for them to carry on, by their example and speech, the proclamation-mission that he started.[17]

15. See also Mark 16:15: "Go into all the world and proclaim the gospel to the whole creation."

16. While the work of Christ is sufficient for all humankind, it is efficient for those who believe (John 3:16; 5:23; 6:29), who are, according to John, the elect (John 6:37, 44; cf. Rom. 8:29–30). This truth may be contained in the oblique statement of "many" in Mark 10:45/Isa. 53:11, 12).

17. Compare the keyword connection "gospel" in 1:14(–15) and 13:10.

Further Analysis of Mark 8:38

Mark 8:38 is a very challenging verse. We will approach it first by briefly recapitulating Jesus' revelation and description of himself as Son of Man. We have already suggested that the self-designation Son of Man holds a central key to finding answers to the self-understanding of Jesus. We have reflected on the fact that Jesus speaks of Isaiah's Servant of Yahweh (Isa. 52:13–53:12) in terms of the humiliated Son of Man (Mark 10:45) who suffers on behalf of his people. Paul will later describe the same truth in terms of the incarnate Son of God becoming a slave who dies on the cross (Phil. 2:5–8).

We also connected the humiliation of Christ with the realization that such humiliation is exactly the way we can be healed from our autonomous existence. What Jesus does in his atonement on our behalf reveals most clearly how severe our state before God really is. The clearest description of the severity of our alienation from God is the extent to which Jesus had to go to heal the breach (Isa. 53:5).

The humbling of Christ and his willingness to suffer is expressed by his "coming in sandals"[18] in order, for example, to wash Peter's feet (John 13:1–20). In Mark 8:38, however, Jesus claims that he will preside as chief judge of the universe and over every soul in this universe. Mark 8:38 claims that the exalted Son of Man will preside over the judgment of Buddha, Plato, Socrates, Confucius, Mohammed, Augustine, Luther, Mao, Hitler, you, and me. He will preside over the judgment of every political leader in the dramatic history of humankind. He will preside as judge over the wise men and scholars of this world. He will preside as judge over the most learned economists this world has ever seen. The very one who kneels to wash Peter's feet is concurrently the exalted Son of Man spoken of in Daniel 7:13–14. On account of this, we can state that "Yahweh, God, comes in sandals."[19] Jesus warns his disciples

18. See John the Baptist's statement in Mark 1:7; cf. 8:31; 10:45.
19. J. S. Bach expresses this truth in his composition "King of Heaven, I Welcome You" composed for Palm Sunday.

in Mark 8:38 that he, as the Danielic Son of Man, will be the judge over all creation.

It is very important to realize that the Son of Man's humiliation and exaltation, which generate a pattern for the disciples to imitate, in this way also create a new community. The very personal claim of Jesus on our lives is an invitation to join the redeemed and renewed community of God. The individual's redemption of Christ creates community. It is a transformed community that is to be "salt and light." While it is appropriate that we emphasize the call of Jesus on each individual person's life, we must always realize that the new community of God is the goal of Christ's redemption.[20]

Holistic Confession and Proclamation of Christ

We have discussed what it means to confess Christ (Mark 8:38). Now we shall pay closer attention to how we are to confess Christ in a biblically based manner.

The widespread way of reading Romans 10:14–15 is that the word of the gospel, the good news of salvation in and through Christ, must be communicated exclusively by preaching, teaching, evangelism, etc. It is true and necessary that the gospel message be preached and taught, not just by preachers, evangelists, teachers, elders, and deacons (1 and 2 Tim. and Titus), but by everyone in the congregation: "but in your hearts honor Christ the Lord as holy, always being prepared to make a defense to anyone who asks you for a reason for the hope that is in you; yet do it with gentleness and respect" (1 Peter 3:15). All disciples are called to such proclamation, and must be aware that this is to happen in a holistic way.

Already 1 Peter 3:15 hints at this effect when it combines speaking with a gentle and respectful way of life. The impact of Christ on our lives transforms us and enables us to be holistic

20. Dietrich Bonhoeffer, *Life Together*, trans. John W. Doberstein (New York: Harper & Row, 1954), 77, 86, 88–89, makes it plain that the purity of the community depends on the purity of the individual members. And it is only in God-given purity that we are salt and light in our communities and societies.

witnesses. We are called to live holistic lives in which all areas of our being are transparent and exposed to the triune God. Furthermore, we are to be "open books" to a few fellow disciples as well.

Essentially, holistic proclamation is speech in the context of our entire lives, individually and communally. We are called to confess and reflect Christ in the context of our thoughts, feelings, relationships, handling of money, and moral challenges. In holistic confession, speech is embedded in the totality of our lives, which proclaims the gospel, reflecting and confessing Christ. Our lives and our speech together confess who Jesus is and what he accomplishes in the reversal of the universal collapse of God-dependent relationships.

Holistic confession means that Jesus has entered our lives to transform us thoroughly. He does not merely transform our words, our activities dedicated to church life, or our allegiance to moral laws. The gift of salvation through Christ's atonement marks the start of our transformation, affecting all areas of individual and communal life. To become holistic witnesses of Jesus we must break away from many cultural habits, world views that deny God,[21] and behaviors that oppose the gospel and thus the will of the triune God. These include, e.g., racial prejudice, the ongoing gender war, dishonesty and injustice in the workplace and the family, and much more.

Holistic witness means to break away from a self-centered and self-serving way of life in exchange for a God-surrendered, God-serving life. We must break away from anything that puts distance between us and God, even if it means putting distance between us and those around us who entice us away from God. It means that we willingly surrender to God's guidance and to any necessary suffering that he allows in our lives. We must realize that God uses suffering to purify and to shape our individual and collective witness.

To become holistic followers of Jesus, we must learn to appropriate Jesus' presence and work and the characteristics of the

21. Such as materialistic naturalism. For helpful detail on various worldviews, see Nancy Pearcey, *Total Truth* (Wheaton: Crossway, 2004).

Holy Spirit dwelling in us. We must learn to depend on God for everything.

The call to proclamation in Romans 10:14–15 is to be combined with a surrendered, transformed, and tested character. Second Corinthians 6:1–13 impressively illustrates this all-inclusive transformation. While Paul makes it clear that faith comes from hearing the proclaimed word, he states unmistakably in this passage that such preaching demands surrender of the whole man.

As is well known, the Corinthian church was struggling in many ways. Its core problem may be summarized as an insatiable hunger for status (in the areas of authority, economic standing, societal honor, personal rights in lawsuits, sexual relationships, etc.). Furthermore, the society was relatively rootless and shaped considerably by a mind-over-matter, Neoplatonic worldview.

In contrast to all of this, Paul describes in 2 Corinthians 6:1–13 what sort of "living letter" (cf. 2 Cor. 3:3) he is. He suffers much external opposition, he experiences God's merciful intervention, and his character is being purified in the process. While Paul confesses Christ, God cleans Paul's secret closets. He is being purified by the fire of adversity, satanic opposition, and hatred. As he humbly surrenders to the guidance and protection of his merciful Lord, further cleansing occurs, so that his witness becomes increasingly more transparent and pure. The self-centered and proud Corinthian church was in need of the very best minister, a transparent servant of Christ, a man tried in the fire of adversity, pain, and rejection.

This is precisely the portrait of holistic witness that many young people all around the globe yearn for: thoughtful, authentic people who submit to absolute truth in a humble way, while realizing that they are in much need of growth themselves. A holistic witness is given by persons and communities who are thoughtful, open with their own weaknesses, and boasting in the weighty grace of God and not in themselves. A holistic witness is someone in and through whom Christ becomes visible.

We are called to reflect God's transforming grace in our dysfunctional families, churches, friendships, work, worldview, disciplines, etc. We will not be perfect by any means, but we will be changed.

As already mentioned, this holistic approach to individual lives has corporate consequences. The centrality of the presence of the triune God, the proclamation of the good news, conversion, and growth in godliness are fundamental. Nevertheless, as in concentric circles, social, political, economic, and cultural challenges are also addressed as consistent consequences in a holistic way. Disciples of Christ are thus called to be living letters holistically (2 Cor. 3:3).

Conclusion

The basis of discipleship is Jesus' atoning and healing resolution of the existential double crisis of self-perception (autonomy) and God-perception (alienation from the triune God). On this basis, Jesus, according to Mark, teaches, exemplifies, and enables eight core character traits in each and every disciple throughout the ages. As a consequence of radical transformation effected by Christ and mediated by the Holy Spirit, each follower will increasingly: (1) surrender to God and do his will; (2) believe and trust; (3) pray; (4) watch over and guard his/her heart; (5) be humbly serving and teachable; (6) forgive; (7) withstand temptation and persecution; and 8) confess Christ to all humanity.

These core character traits mark each follower as being shaped and transformed by Christ. They are to be understood as the fruit of Christ's impact, *not* as spiritual disciplines that followers of Christ emulate in their own strength.

While we have emphasized that there are many other consequences of Jesus' impact in the lives of his disciples, we note that these eight characteristics lie at the heart of true existence. We might say that they constitute foundational building blocks of Christ's new humanity in all spheres of society.

8

A Reciprocal Approach
to Discipleship

WE HAVE TRACED in chapters 6–7 the eight core characteristics arising from Jesus' tri-polar resolution to the double crisis. Christ's call to holistic discipleship constitutes the launch of the new humanity in dependence upon him. The journey of growth is by no means merely individual or personal, but, very centrally, reciprocal and communal in nature. Regardless of the question of how the process of making disciples is envisioned, those who disciple and those who are being discipled always enter a relationship of reciprocity. And this can already be seen in Mark.

At the very foundation of discipleship lies the fact that Jesus never trains merely one disciple by himself or herself. Rather, from the start, Jesus engages a group of disciples. Immediately, then, there is not only a teaching dimension between Jesus and the respective disciple, but also a horizontal reciprocal teaching and learning dynamic among the disciples. Because Jesus is present among his disciples today by means of his Spirit, that same pattern is perpetuated in the twenty-first century.

For the original disciples, being sent out by Christ two by two, learning discipleship in the group of the Twelve, and being shaped by Christ sets up a pattern of reciprocal learning and mutual teaching which is not terminated with Jesus' physical departure. The transformation process started by Jesus sets in motion a rhythm of give and take, a teach-and-be-taught dynamic, a mirroring phenomenon. In this each disciple sees the others and is seen by the others moving toward growth in internalizing the double crisis, internalizing its tri-polar resolution in Christ, and in manifesting the core characteristics. Far from learning the lesson once and for all, reciprocity ensures ongoing communal internalization of Christ's impact. Transformation thus happens in the process of life to the one who disciples as well as to the one who is being discipled. This process includes following the commission to make disciples.[1]

We can trace this phenomenon as we briefly look beyond Mark to the rest of the New Testament, focusing particularly on Matthew 28:19–20; Acts 9:10–27; 10:1–48; Philippians 2:1–5; and Ephesians 4:11–16. Surprisingly, we will find that the Great Commission in Matthew 28:19–20 leads us into a process of reciprocity in discipleship. This means that we are learning from each other wherever we are. It is one of God's tools for the transformation of our hearts in the global body of Christ.

The well-known Great Commission must especially be viewed in a reciprocal rather than a traditional unilateral way. In the Great Commission, Jesus sends his thoroughly trained disciples out to teach and to learn, to give and to receive, to shape and to be shaped, to disciple and to be discipled. In Matthew 28:19–20 Jesus says: "Therefore go and make disciples of all nations, baptizing them into the name of the Father and of the Son and of the Holy Spirit, and teaching them to obey everything I have commanded you." We tend to read the call of the Great Commission in terms of a unilateral, one-way dynamic: The disciples make disciples, and by implication, I, as a disciple, make you into a disciple.

In reality, however, this corresponds neither to the biblical evidence nor to real life. What we often overlook is the fact that discipleship dynamics are reciprocal in terms of both biblical evidence and experience. In discipleship reciprocity we discover an active give-and-take dynamic, which is far from one-way. Rather,

1. While Mark does not contain an explicit commission to "make disciples" (in contrast to Matt. 28:18–20), the entire book is a call to discipleship narrating how Jesus had the authority to call disciples and how he went about doing it.

discipleship dynamics are characterized by learning together in dependence upon Christ what it means to grow as his disciples. It means mutually living under his true lordship, finding God as the actual center of our individual and corporate lives, and learning to see ourselves with God-centered peripheral vision.

More recent research, including the work of Christopher Wright,[2] reflects this shift in the correct direction of mission by coining more appropriate terms to describe the biblical reality. We encounter such terms as reciprocal partnerships or missional partners, thus leaving behind the old centrifugal dynamic of mission.[3]

Before we consider the biblical basis for the reality of discipleship reciprocity, let us clarify that the reciprocity process is not about establishing or determining truth. God has reliably revealed himself and his overall mission in redemptive-historical fashion, climaxing in the sending of his beloved eternal Son. The prophetic and apostolic witness of truth in the Old and New Testaments has been canonically established. What I mean by discipleship reciprocity then is the fact that all of us, beginning with the apostles, need to grow in understanding and living out the ramifications of that biblical witness. We thus stress that reciprocity is not an endorsement of a relative truth about God. Instead, it affirms that absolute truth resides with the self-revealing God, so that we, in reciprocal discipleship relationships, continuously submit to God, his Word, and his work in his people. Growth in discipleship thus means: corporate learning and embodying of the depth of the gospel under the true headship of Christ, who affords us access to the Trinity.

Living as Christ's disciples is a process of becoming. Paul often speaks about that process in terms of dying to self and becoming alive to Christ (Rom. 6:10–11) and putting to death the works of the flesh (Gal. 5:19; Col. 3:5), that is, becoming increasingly Christlike. Jesus speaks about it in terms of denying oneself

2. Christopher J. H. Wright, *The Mission of God: Unlocking the Bible's Grand Narrative* (Downers Grove, IL: InterVarsity, 2006).
3. Ibid., 24ff.

and following him (Mark 8:34). Jesus challenges his disciples to internalize who they really are in God's eyes and who God truly is (Mark 8:17–21). John speaks about progressive discipleship in terms of continuously walking in the light and life of Jesus (John 8:12) and depending on Jesus as branches depend on the vine (John 15:1ff.). All of this points toward a growth process.

Biblical Examples of Discipleship Reciprocity[4]

Acts 9:10–27

In this passage we have a reciprocal discipleship relationship between two individuals, Ananias and Paul. Note here the instruction to Ananias, the follower of Jesus: go to the house of Judas on Straight Street and ask for a man from Tarsus called Saul. This instruction can be seen as a particular application of the Great Commission (Matt. 28:19–20; Acts 9:10–11). Note further the strong resistance from Ananias (Acts 9:13): "Lord," Ananias answered, "I have heard many reports about this man and all the harm he has done to your saints in Jerusalem. And he has come here with authority from the chief priests to arrest all who call on your name." In other words, Ananias says: "Jesus, please be reasonable; do not overinterpret the great commission."[5]

Note then the surprising breakthrough in Acts 9:17. Ananias says: "Brother Saul."[6] This incident demonstrates that mature disciples (Ananias, Barnabas, and others) had to learn that Jesus' Great Commission was meant to break through many citadel-like barriers of culture, language, nations, ethnicities, religions, and worldviews.

---

4. This important dimension of these texts was brought to my attention by Tim Baldwin.

5. A later example of disciples attempting to limit the extent of the Great Commission is in Acts 9:26: When Saul came to Jerusalem, "he tried to join the disciples, but they were all afraid of him, not believing that he really was a disciple." The disciples and apostles in Jerusalem were uncertain about the extent to which the Great Commission applied.

6. See again the Jerusalem parallel in Acts 9:27: "but Barnabas took him and brought him to the apostles."

In this instance we notice that both Ananias and Saul learn under the headship of Christ what it means to be a disciple. Not only does the convert Paul begin to learn but also the mature disciple Ananias grows and develops in following Christ. In the process, former enemies of the faith become reconciled brothers.

Acts 10:1–48

In this passage we have an example of reciprocal discipleship between small groups of people: Peter with six companions on the one hand, and Cornelius, the centurion, with his household and friends on the other. In the unfolding narrative, Peter progressively defiles himself ceremonially by living in the house of an unclean tanner, by being confronted with the command to eat unclean food, and then by going into the house of an unclean Gentile.

Following Peter's mature stance in his Pentecost and temple speeches (Acts 2–3), including his many courageous acts surrounding the beginning of the messianic church in Jerusalem and beyond, we might get the impression that the thoroughly trained disciple and apostle Peter was fully matured as a follower of Christ. We might think that by now he knows the significance, extent, and application of the gospel. We would consider him fully fit to make disciples. Based on Acts 10:1–48, however, this is not so; when it comes to living out the ramifications of the gospel, the great disciple and apostle Peter is still a learner. Note the way God interweaves the lives of Cornelius and Peter. They both learn, grow, and develop in their respective ways. In fact, the great apostle might have more to learn than the centurion! Shockingly, Peter has to learn that Christ's atonement is fully sufficient even to cleanse an unclean, God-fearing Gentile (see Eph. 2:11–21).

This reciprocity in discipleship extends to church life and, by implication, to church planting as well as to interchurch partnerships. This holds true because church plants and interchurch partnerships are extensions of personal and small group discipleship. Let it suffice here to offer a third example.

Philippians 2:1–5

In this passage, Paul issues a call to reciprocal discipleship between the Philippian church and his team. The appeal reflects a growing relationship between Paul, his team, and the Philippian church which he so dearly loves. This text may be familiar to you. Listen to it from the vantage point of reciprocity. Paul encourages the Philippian Christians to join in the growth in Christ:

> If you have any encouragement from being united with Christ, if any comfort from his love, if any fellowship with the Spirit, if any tenderness and compassion, then make my joy complete by being like-minded, having the same love, being one in spirit and purpose. Do nothing out of selfish ambition or vain conceit, but in humility consider others better than yourselves. Each of you should look not only to your own interests, but also to the interests of others. Your attitude should be the same as that of Christ Jesus . . .

Note Paul's emphasis on "make my joy complete." In other words: "let us, together, grow in that kind of humility." With this reciprocal tone there is no room for spiritual unilateralism, for a one-way approach to discipleship. Rather, Paul submits to the same call for maturity with which he exhorts the Philippian Christians. The one who disciples others is always first and foremost challenged to grow himself in what he seeks to convey to another. When Paul says: "Do nothing out of selfish ambition or vain conceit, but in humility consider others better than yourselves," he is submitting himself to that standard as well. In this profound text we find a humble and reciprocal encouragement toward mutual service which exemplifies a core characteristic of discipleship.[7]

Conclusion

What is so liberating about reciprocal discipleship is the fact that the discipler does not stand in the center. Rather, God is at

7. See pp. 112–14.

the center. We all, individually and corporately, move toward God in the process of discipleship. We learn the deeper truth of God's own mission when we enter into sincere discipleship reciprocity. This means that we need to continue to learn to break through cultural, ethnic, national, and language barriers to make room for growth of the worldwide community of faith. If we align ourselves to God's mission of reconciliation and restoration, we enter the arena of God's work in individuals and churches in many places around the world. We all participate in a grand process, serving reciprocally as contributors. We enter into the focus of God's purposes in and through Christ.

We must recognize that today the commission to go and make disciples happens *from* all corners of the earth *to* all corners of the earth, which necessarily implies reciprocity. This dynamic creates missional and reciprocal discipleship, through which we grow in giving and receiving, in shaping and being shaped, in following Christ and being discipled. As a consequence, we are no more at the center of what is happening.[8] Rather, we all arrange ourselves, by teaching and learning, around the greatness of God himself. The center of the world is God and his grand mission all over the world. The center is his transformation in and through his people all over the world. We are dependent upon people of different regions, colors, ethnicities, religious backgrounds, and socio-economic strata in order to learn what it really means to be Christ's disciples.

Why is this so? We need such dependence in order to grow in discipleship, individually and communally. Without these enriching reciprocity opportunities, we, as individuals and as communities, will not learn as Christ desires. Furthermore, we will be deprived of growing as an equipping, receiving, teaching, learning, stewarding, and listening body. We must therefore ask ourselves: do we intentionally welcome being discipled by other individuals and communities submitted to Christ? We can mature greatly through them and their testimony of God's discipleship in their

8. See Nelson Jennings, *God the Real Superpower: Rethinking Our Role in Missions* (Phillipsburg, NJ: P&R Publishing, 2007).

midst. They are as much messengers to us as we are messengers to them. Just as God uses others in our lives so that we grow, he uses representatives of ethnic minorities, other countries, church plants, and church partnerships, to mature us and to mature each individual and group.

We may ask representatives of other communities what they have learned from God and find out what they are struggling with. We may ask them what strengths and weaknesses they see in us and our churches. We may ask them what we need to learn from them in order to grow. They must be empowered to contribute to our process of growth in Christ as much as we need to contribute to their process of growth. When individuals and communities enter into partnerships with individuals and churches in other areas, a rich reciprocity ensues that provides life for all parties involved. God uses this to mature all participants. To avoid entering into the reciprocity of discipleship seriously impoverishes the growth of the individual and the community. God's claim on our lives is to mature in him together.

As a closing exercise, consider Ephesians 4:11–16, addressed to a group of Christians who are exhorted to grow up in Christ, with a framework of reciprocal discipleship in a worldwide partnership. Before reading the text, think of individuals and communities in different parts of the world:

> It was he who gave some to be apostles, some to be prophets, some to be evangelists, and some to be pastors and teachers, to prepare God's people for works of service, so that the body of Christ may be built up until we all reach unity in the faith and in the knowledge of the Son of God and become mature, attaining to the whole measure of the fullness of Christ. Then we [together] will no longer be infants, tossed back and forth by the waves, and blown here and there by every wind of teaching and by the cunning and craftiness of men in their deceitful scheming. Instead, [each one] speaking the truth in love, we will in all things grow up into him who is the Head, that is, Christ. From him the whole body, joined and held together by every supporting ligament, grows and builds itself up in love, as each part does its work.

Following Mark's Call in the Twenty-first Century

As a deer pants for flowing streams, so pants my soul for you, O God. (Ps. 42:1)

Come to me, all who labor and are heavy laden, and I will give you rest. Take my yoke upon you, and learn from me, for I am gentle and lowly in heart, and you will find rest for your souls. For my yoke is easy, and my burden is light. (Matt. 11:28–30)

And having come this far, true spirituality—the Christian life—flows on into the total culture. (Francis Schaeffer)[1]

Introduction: A Definition of Contemporary Spirituality[2]

Pursuing some form of spirituality is once again fashionable both in the United States and in Western Europe. In 2001, the Archbishop of York, David Hope, said: "There are deep spiritual yearnings, longings. Large numbers of people say they pray. But they are not into religion" (by which Hope means organized religion).[3] A report of the Evangelical Covenant Church (IFFEC)

1. Francis Schaeffer, *True Spirituality* (Carol Stream, IL: Tyndale House, 1971), 180.
2. My daughter, Katharine Gleich, researched elements of contemporary German spirituality while studying at the University of Heidelberg. Aspects of her findings have found their way into the following discussion.
3. See www.ucgstp.org/lit/gn/gn033/world.html; accessed 1/15/2008.

in Berlin in May 2007 stated: "There are signs of increasing spiritual interest throughout Europe as secularism fails to address the spiritual yearnings of the heart."[4] There are indications in the United States which point to an increased interest in some form of spirituality, at times in connection with some type of faith community. However, the substance of this interest is difficult to describe. In these and many other contexts, spirituality is often mentioned, but less often explained. It is necessary, then, to define our use of the term spirituality in the current context.

By spirituality we mean here primarily transcendent knowledge, wisdom, feeling, intuition, and experience. In recent decades, however, the term has increasingly been used to describe any search for significant meaning within or without a person. Today spirituality thus does not necessarily mean that a person is pursuing something or someone outside the physical world. Furthermore, we must take note of the contemporary distinction between religious (participating in organized religion) and spiritual pursuits, the latter being often synonymous with a personal or corporate search for meaning. On account of this contemporary blurring of the lines between transcendent and immanent spheres of reality, we will use the term spirituality in this broader sense, while still primarily focusing on the traditional sense of a search for the transcendent. Though we will not directly address the search for physical, intellectual, and emotional immanent meaning, such as sex, power, money, knowledge, technological advance, fame, and the like, the many paths of spirituality discussed below do have relevance to those who search merely for such immanent meaning.

The State of Contemporary Spirituality

For the sake of clarity, we group spiritual trends in various Western (pop) cultures in the following three broad categories:

4. See www.covchurch.org/cov/news/itemm5568; accessed 1/15/2008.

Spiritual Yearnings

By spiritual yearnings we mean the longing for transcendent (or immanent) knowledge, wisdom, feeling, and the like, including the search for moral absolutes, which leads one beyond oneself. These spiritual yearnings may be expressed in the following variety of ways:

- A yearning for free expression of self, emotions, and feelings, especially in the artistic world. Confinement to the mundane appears to stifle growth and true expression of self. This yearning can, for example, take the form of seeking chance circumstances as a possible opportunity to realize dreams and to find liberation from normalcy, thus capturing the imagination. Many forms of adventure, spontaneous romance, and experimentation can be mentioned here.[5] Representatives of these yearnings seek to tease out something transcendent in life. Oliver Stone's statement represents one aspect of this: "I don't want integrity to block my creative growth."[6]

- A yearning for supernatural powers, even in the form of spiritism and Satanism. More than in past decades, many people are being drawn into involvement with spiritism, Satanism, ancestor worship (seeking the guidance of deceased parents in their surviving children's lives), and superstition. In the absence of a transcendent arbitrator over good and evil, spirituality is viewed as neutral. Anything transcendent is valuable.

- A longing for community and relationships as potential spheres of spiritual experience. There is a desire to belong to a group or some form of a family, a longing for rootedness,

---

5. See, e.g., many French films, such as *Amélie* (2001). The popular Georgian/British pop star Katie Melua sings the following as a refrain in her love song "If You Were a Sailboat" (2007): "Sometimes I believe in fate, but the chances we create always seem to ring more true; you took a chance on loving me, I took a chance on loving you." A resulting despair is found in Leonard Cohen's hauntingly brilliant song "Hallelujah" (1984).

6. Cornelius Plantinga, *Not the Way It's Supposed to Be: A Breviary of Sin* (Grand Rapids: Eerdmans, 1995), 28.

tradition, and life story. These desires are combined with openness to diversity. One sphere for these longings is still the natural family and/or a community of love. This is happening despite and parallel to a widespread collapse of family and community structures.[7] In these groups there is the opportunity to be known and to experience intimacy, perceived as potential carriers of transcendent meaning. A further element here is the return to tradition and ritual as yet another opportunity to experience some form of spirituality.[8] The attraction of Roman Catholicism[9] and (Eastern) Orthodox traditions, with their appeals to mind, soul, and senses, reflects a hunger among spiritual seekers both for the intellectual pursuit of the wisdom found in centuries-old traditions, as well as the yearning for holistic worship, community, and transformation.

- A need for authentic, nonabusive authority-models. This need is widespread and may be identified as a universal yearning among those who have experienced heavy-handed, abusive authority-models.

- A yearning for authentic, traditional transcendence, leading to true meaning and transformative experience. One expression can be seen in the ongoing search for finding solace in westernized Buddhism, especially in dealing with suffering and pain in order to achieve experiential, quasi-transcendent serenity.

7. The spiritual ramifications are intriguing. See the Eberstadt theory for Europe: the decay of the natural family is associated with the decay of spirituality (Mary Eberstadt, "How the West Really Lost God," in *Policy Review* 143 [1 July 2007]: 3–20). Eberstadt's thesis is not that the "God is dead" theology led to the decay of the churches, but rather that the disintegration of the natural family and reduced family growth did so. Her thesis is only partially convincing though, since the "God is dead" theology runs parallel to the decay of natural family structures. There is thus a philosophical component to this decline as well.

8. Jay Tolson, "A Return to Tradition: Going Back to Traditional Roots in Catholic, Protestant, Jewish, and Muslim Circles," *U.S. News and World Report* (Dec. 24, 2007): 42–48. Tolson questions whether the revival of Islamic rituals in Islam is a return to *traditional* Islam or going to the "highly puritanical reformist Islam associated with Wahabi and Salafist teachings" (44), which some Islamic scholars do not identify as traditional Islam.

9. Especially through the late John Paul II.

- A desire to understand the world's origin and structure, its laws and purpose. This understanding is, at times, meant to affect the world and the environment for the better. As in all ages, there is an ongoing search for and promise of an ultimate harmony between the natural sciences (origin of the universe and man) and the transcendent (cf., e.g., Francis Bacon).

- A longing for simplicity and spiritually rewarding experiences and exercises. Elements of this can be found among various Christian, Jewish, and Muslim groups, as well as among Quakers, in Mormonism, and among Jehovah's Witnesses. These circles often offer straightforward and simple guidelines to moral and outward (at times religious) behavior as the spiritual focus of life. Frequently there is a call to social action, activism, charity, and the like. Spirituality is here often synonymous with communal and altruistic action.

Spiritual Self-Disclosures

By spiritual self-disclosures we mean the honest admission of brokenness and needs in the pursuit of transcendent (or immanent) spirituality. These self-disclosures may be expressed in the following variety of ways:

- The courage of openly expressing the problems of pain, suffering, evil, grief, isolation, fear, death (vs. feeling the weight and value of existence), and in decrying an ugly brokenness (vs. the beauty and ability of man). We note a pronounced, cynical reaction to alienation, existential loneliness[10] (selfishness), meaninglessness, anger, depression, and rejection of materialism. There is a pervasive and restless resignation and the feeling of being a victim, which often drives a culture of death, combined with an intense sensitivity to psychological and physical suffering.

10. See, e.g., the British band Radiohead.

137

Disorientation, guilt, shame, and failure are frequent consequences. The yearning to come to terms with such pervasive and existential pain in the experience of life appears to be an important launching pad for multidirectional spiritual searches.

- The willingness to submit to fate, resigning to that which appears to be predetermined anyway, or seeking transcendent, impersonal guidance. These sentiments can go hand in hand with the rejection of responsibility. Astrology and New Age beliefs have been long-standing expressions of this form of spirituality.[11]

- The admission to being unashamedly self-absorbed and independent, by pursuing an endless string of diversions and spiritual entertainments.[12]

Spiritual Self-Assertions

By spiritual self-assertions we mean human claims in the realm of transcendent (or immanent) spirituality, including the limiting of reality to the nonsupernatural sphere.[13] These self-assertions may be expressed in the following variety of ways:

- Formulating transcendent beliefs subjectively and experientially and thus rejecting absolute truth(s). This form of spiritual self-assertion can be seen, for example, in

11. We find here a colorful mosaic of irrationalism, passivity, astrology, vegetarianism, asceticism, psychic healing, mysticism, etc. It is possible to connect the pursuit of a quasi-Gnostic, speculative, nonhistorical, oracle-like wisdom-spirituality with the New Age movement.

12. See Richard Winter, *Still Bored in a Culture of Entertainment* (Downers Grove, IL: InterVarsity, 2002).

13. By this we mean the explicit philosophical or experiential rejection of transcendence. We intentionally include the postulate of rationalistic immanence in that it attempts to make a definitive anti-transcendent statement, effectively elevating the human mind to function as the spiritual arbitrator for assessing the universe, after exploring transcendence (see especially I. Kant and now the New Atheism). Naturalistic materialism is one branch of this, issuing, e.g., in theories of naturalistic evolution, at times seeking spiritual meaning therein. For further insights, see Gerhard Maier, *Biblical Hermeneutics*, 1st English edition, trans. Robert Yarbrough (Grand Rapids: Crossway, 1994).

contemporary pluralism and postmodernism, both of which represent a reaction to the failure of the rationalistic program since the Enlightenment.[14] Life is seen as a journey, a narrative, an authentic story. A characteristic aspect is that postmodernism moves from the autonomy and normative view of reason (modernism) to the autonomy and normative view of self and personal experience.[15]

- Being unwilling to carry responsibility and simultaneously breaking free from top-down, heavy-handed authority structures.

- Reducing religious texts to mere spiritual literature, pursuing an ahistorical, exclusively literary approach to ancient religious records.[16]

14. See Alister McGrath, *A Passion for Truth: The Intellectual Coherence of Evangelicalism* (Downers Grove, IL: InterVarsity, 1996). Pluralism removes the constraints of modernism while postmodernism furnishes a new framework. Regarding pluralism, McGrath states: "Claims by any one group or individual to have any exclusive hold on 'truth' are thus treated as the intellectual equivalent of Fascism. This form of pluralism is strongly prescriptive, seeking to lay down what may be believed, rather than merely describe what is believed. Significantly, . . . the first casualty of the prescriptive pluralist agenda is truth"(206). Pluralism and individualism seem to go hand in hand. Postmodernism builds on pluralistic principles: Jean Francois Lyotard claims that postmodernism "refines our sensitivity to differences and reinforces our ability to tolerate the incommensurable" (*La condition postmoderne*, trans. Geoff Bennington and Brian Massumi [Minneapolis: University of Minnesota Press, 1979, 1984]). McGrath characterizes the movement from modernism to postmodernism as follows: While modernism values purpose, design, hierarchy, centering, selection, and facts, postmodernism now values, respectively, chance, anarchy, dispersal, combination, and story (*Passion for Truth*, 184).

15. The attempt of a synthesis of modernism and postmodernism is noticeable in Daniel Pink's influential book *A Whole New Mind: Why Right-Brainers Will Rule the Future* (New York: Riverhead Books, 2006), see especially 65–66. He identifies six aptitudes to complement left-brain directed reasoning (i.e., much of modernism). According to Pink, human beings in the twenty-first century need to learn to complement functionality with *beauty and emotion*; arguments with a *"compelling narrative"*; (analytical) focus with *interdisciplinary synthesis*; logical thought with *caring relationships*; serious engagement with *lighthearted play*; material gain with *"purpose, transcendence, and spiritual fulfillment"* (67).

16. A characteristic representative of this ongoing trend is Jack Miles' "narrative theology" in his work *God: A Biography* (New York: Vintage Books, 1995). He states: "I write here about the life of the Lord God as—and only as—the protagonist of a classic of world literature; namely the Hebrew Bible or Old Testament. I do not write about (though I certainly do not write against) the Lord God as the object of religious belief. I do not attempt, as theology does, to make an original statement about God as an extra-literary reality" (10).

• Asserting self in the midst of a vacuum of meaning.[17] Chantal Delsol's analysis points to a great double disillusionment in Europe: the loss of rootedness in the Christian faith on the one hand, and its failed utopian replacements of communism and fascism on the other. The situation is comparable to Icarus, fallen with damaged wings and full of self-doubt. Delsol speaks of the design feature of man's longing for absolutes. However, there is no coherent ideology currently available by which to satisfy man's longing. Delsol states: "In general, our contemporary cannot imagine for what cause he would sacrifice his life because he does not know what his life means."

• Asserting oneself in the midst of competing world religions. The resurgence of Islam is the most conspicuous element here. In the Global South we note, for example, the search for transcendent experiences combined with the parallel phenomenon of religious competition.[18] Religious self-assertions experience push-backs both in the Christian and Muslim spheres. There is a curious answer to the current rationalistic self-assertion in the West in the world of Islam. We note two aspects: (1) the Qur'an's critique of Judaism and Christianity runs parallel to a rationalistic Western critique of the Judeo-Christian heritage, and (2) a discernible enlightened movement among Muslim thinkers and most ardent opponents of radical Islamic militancy.[19] The latter constitutes an

17. Chantal Delsol, *Icarus Fallen: The Search for Meaning in an Uncertain World*, ed. and trans. Robin Dick (Wilmington, DE: ISI Books, 2003). Delsol is a professor of philosophy at the University of Marne-la-Vallée in Paris. Note this phenomenon particularly in Europe. As with modernism, this expression of what I would call "numbed spirituality" is the result of rejecting traditional transcendence, and therefore must be mentioned here.

18. Philip Jenkins, *The Next Christendom: The Coming of Global Christianity* (Oxford University Press, 2002) and *The New Faces of Christianity: Believing the Bible in the Global South* (Oxford University Press, 2006). In general, self-assertion may occur in the areas of biblical literalism and culturalism (tribalism), since life has to be lived in the context of competing religions (Islam, Hinduism, Christianity).

19. See, e.g., Ayaan Jirsi Ali, *Infidel* (New York: Free Press, 2007 [Eng. transl.]), esp. 281–82.

inner-Islamic struggle which is comparable to the rise of enlightenment thought in Europe in the late eighteenth century.

- Demanding objective certainty by means of rationalism and/or naturalistic, modern science (see the New Atheism). While this area appears, on the surface, not to belong to spiritual self-assertions, it qualifies in fact as a rationalistic, after-the-effect rejection of the transcendent. There is a continuing, modernist rejection of an ultimate, transcendent point of reference. It is anti-spiritual in the sense that it makes definitive statements against transcendence in the traditional sense of the word, after exploring traditional transcendent options.[20] It is thus necessary to include it in our discussion here.[21] Modernism postulates the autonomy and normative standard of reason.[22] There is a strong contemporary strand of modernism, not only in the form of scientific naturalism (Richard Dawkins and the New Atheism)[23] but also in philosophical/ethical

20. See the rationalistic arguments against any reasonable proof of the existence of God in Immanuel Kant's *Critique of Pure Reason* (1781).

21. The intellectual discourse regarding the transcendent versus mere immanent reality increasingly reflects the polarization of extremes (see "The Polarization of Extremes," *Chronicle of Higher Education* [Dec. 14, 2007]). There is a focus on what members of a particular interest group want to hear; there is less openness to hear opposing views; members of a particular group are self-assured and dismissive of anything that opposes the views of their group.

22. The core of rationalism consists of: (a) French skepticism: Rene Descartes (1596–1650) advancing indubitable mental abilities and principal, fundamental doubt and accepting only irreducible certainty ("cogito, ergo sum"= "I think, therefore I am"); (b) David Hume's empirical skepticism; and (c) German rationalism (Immanuel Kant, *Critique of Pure Reason*) advancing the autonomy and normative character of reason and the impossibility of knowing "the thing in itself."

23. The contemporary so-called "New Atheism" is partially a form of anti-theism, especially concerning the God of the Bible. See Richard Dawkins, *The God Delusion* (New York: Bantam, 2006); Sam Harris, *The End of Faith: Religion, Terror, and the Future of Reason* (New York: Norton, repr. 2005); Sam Harris, *Letter to a Christian Nation* (New York: Random House, 2006); Christopher Hitchens, *God Is Not Great: How Religion Poisons Everything* (New York: Twelve Books, 2007); Michel Onfray, *Atheist Manifesto: The Case Against Christianity, Judaism, and Islam* (New York: Arcade Books, English ed. 2005); Victor J. Stenger, *God, The Failed Hypothesis: How Science Shows That God Does Not Exist* (Amherst, NY: Prometheus Books, 2007). Counter-arguments against this New Atheism include: Robert Royal, *The God That Did Not Fail: How Religion Built and Sustains the West* (New York: Encounter Books, 2006); Michael Novak, "Lonely Atheists

(Jürgen Habermas) and religious (Bart Ehrman; Elaine Pagels; Gerd Lüdemann; Hans Küng; Muslim intellectuals) rationalism.

The Connection between Elements of Contemporary Spirituality and Discipleship Dynamics in Mark

Introductory Reflections

As we have seen in chapters 1–7, the Gospel of Mark displays a stable interrelationship between literary form, historical setting, and its message, as indicated in the following diagram:

Fig. 10.1. The unity of form, history, and message in Mark

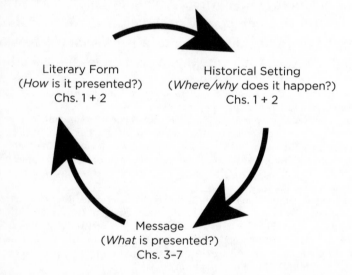

Literary Form
(*How* is it presented?)
Chs. 1 + 2

Historical Setting
(*Where/why* does it happen?)
Chs. 1 + 2

Message
(*What* is presented?)
Chs. 3–7

This stable interrelationship has to be transferred to our contemporary world and life while retaining the integrity of the initial interrelationship in Mark. In other words, we must move from the stable interrelationship as a norm to contemporary appli-

of the Global Village," *National Review* (March 19, 2007); Alister McGrath, *The Twilight of Atheism: The Rise and Fall of Disbelief in the Modern World* (New York: Doubleday, 2004); and John Lennox, *God's Undertaker: Has Science Buried God?* (Oxford: Lion, 2009).

cation as *normans*, which is Latin for "something to be shaped by a norm" (chapter 9), as indicated in this diagram:

Fig. 10.2. Literary sensitivity, historical setting, and "message" in contemporary spiritualties

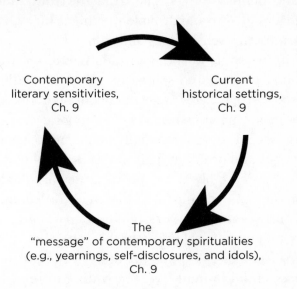

Contemporary literary sensitivities, Ch. 9

Current historical settings, Ch. 9

The "message" of contemporary spiritualities (e.g., yearnings, self-disclosures, and idols), Ch. 9

In the process of relating discipleship dynamics to elements of contemporary spirituality, we must keep this norm-triad intact while making it relevant to our contemporary situation on three levels: our sensitivity to literary forms (e.g., is a bios-story account relevant today?); our current historical setting; and the message of contemporary spiritualities, with which our setting is combined and intertwined.

Before we proceed, a few remarks concerning the literary compatibility between Mark as an ancient bios-account and contemporary life will be helpful. It is noteworthy that both Mark and expressions of contemporary spirituality concern themselves not only with mere propositions and concepts but also with the value of life story, life progression, relationships, and maturing in the context of interaction. Jesus does not merely teach a set of naked concepts and principles to be learned and comprehended. Rather, he shapes holistically the whole life of his disciples, in both conceptual and relational ways. The literary genre of bios, describing key aspects of Jesus' life and teaching and his profound interaction with his disciples, leads to a life calling which is conceptually renewed but also, and centrally, relationally embedded in the totality of life. We thus believe that the truth-and-life nexus of Jesus' teaching, life, and disciple-making is highly compatible with contemporary sensitivities and values.

Identifying some of today's fundamental spiritual yearnings, self-disclosures, and self-assertions, especially in North America and Europe, helps us get out of our own subcultures and introduces us to various aspects of contemporary expressions of human existence. They are essentially statements of contemporary spiritual hopes and needs, and display a cluster of nonnegotiable postulates. From a biblical perspective, they are contemporary expressions of human beings as autonomous reflections of a broken yet reminiscent form of original human design.

Jesus, as a member of the eternal Trinity, the one Creator of the universe, addresses human life at its deepest, transcultural, and most essential human level. According to him, the fundamental issues of alienation from God, self, and others must be addressed regardless of race, gender, ethnicity, culture, and social circumstance prior to addressing any other area of life. These fundamental issues operate on a deeper level than many popular expressions of contemporary spirituality sketched above.

Jesus addresses these root alienations in his call to discipleship by leading his disciples into a double crisis concerning self-perception and God-perception. This crisis directly affects the third issue, namely, that of our perception of others.[24] Jesus thus engages human beings in their intense state of yearnings, painful alienations, and hopeless addictions by identifying these things as consequences of our root alienations.[25] According to Jesus, some aspects of contemporary spirituality can be affirmed, some must

24. One of my students, Rick Whitlock, encouraged me particularly to think more about this important dimension.
25. See Cornelius Plantinga Jr., *Not the Way It's Supposed to Be: A Breviary of Sin* (Grand Rapids: Eerdmans, 1995).

be rejected, and some need to be transformed. This reflects the fact that as creatures, we remain, to a degree, image bearers of God despite our alienated state. This means we still reflect characteristics of God, e.g., the ability to self-reflect; the capacity for true, sacrificial love, worship, and artistic expression; theoretical and abstract analysis; and the expression of complex thought sequences in language. Among other purposes, Jesus restores human beings to the original goal of creation, which frees them to walk with and glorify God as he intended.

The eight character formation values mentioned in chapters 6–7 grow out of that new foundation of a reconciled relationship with God and change our understanding of ourselves and others. Yet, the eight core characteristics are still largely independent of cultural particularities. They are fundamental characteristics of God's definition of what it means to be spiritual. They express the character of our Messiah-King[26] and set the tone for all other aspects of life.

Thus, the contents of chapters 4–7 will always need to constitute a foundation for engagement with and transformation of contemporary spirituality. We contend that Jesus' call into a double crisis, his resolution of the crisis, and his engendering core characteristics in his followers constitute universals for people of all ethnicities, races, and cultural particularities prior to engaging specific aspects of contemporary spirituality.

The problem in some Christian circles is that the focus lies on personal spirituality as facilitated by Jesus. But the necessary cultural engagement is missing or underdeveloped, and creation values are not taken seriously enough.[27] Furthermore, Jesus' initial focus on the individual often overshadows the fact that he trained his disciples corporately. Jesus causes a ripple effect that must touch every area of individual and corporate life.

The problem in other circles, however, is the tendency to circumnavigate Jesus' personal claim on an individual level in exchange for

26. This is a key aspect of the kingdom and rule of God.
27. See, e.g., the enduring goodness of creation, leading to concern for environmental issues.

social spiritual concern and action, which fail to address underlying personal problems of human existence. In the following reflections, we hope to avoid both weaknesses and extremes.

Contemporary Spiritualities and the Double Crisis Caused by Jesus

We surmise that Jesus would not comment on any of the expressions of contemporary spirituality noted above before he had called everyone to engage in fundamental reckoning and reflection. He would confront contemporary representatives of various strands of spirituality first and foremost with his searching questions of self-perception and God-perception. Rather than at the outset discrediting people's deep expressions of yearnings, self-disclosures, and self-assertions, Jesus would first give them a set of searching core challenges, the answers to which will affect everything else in their lives. They would be confronted by the profound reciprocity between self-perception and God-perception.

All self-expressions are thus initially valid. However, in being confronted with Jesus' double crisis, representatives of these self-expressions are challenged to give answers to foundational questions of existence.[28] In the end, the double crisis which Jesus sets in motion aims at a deeper level at which these yearnings might serve as a catalyst for seriously seeking to answer Jesus' questions.

Above all, there is a natural point of contact between these self-diagnosed, contemporary reflections and Jesus' question about the disciples' self-perception. This opens a path to connect the contemporary cry of the heart with Jesus' deconstruction as part of his initial call to discipleship. We have already argued that the resolution to humankind's fundamental alienation from God, self, and others is transcultural and common to all peoples.

Various forms of contemporary spirituality correspond, as faint self-disclosures, to the sharp appeal and challenge of Jesus. In his call to discipleship Jesus addresses the defining and fundamental

---

28. Regarding questions of an adequate self-perception, see David Benner's useful *The Gift of Being Yourself: The Sacred Call to Self-Discovery* (Downers Grove, IL: Inter-Varsity, 2004).

issues of human existence, raising identity and perception questions which are, to a certain degree, echoed in contemporary spiritualities.

The guiding core question will always be: is self-dependence or God-dependence furthered here? Is God glorified in his design of creation and redemption, or is someone or something being idolized, locked into a deformed state? Elements of contemporary spirituality may thus be adopted, rejected, or transformed and restored.

Jesus' double question of "who do you perceive yourself to be?" and "who do you perceive God to be?" takes spiritual yearnings and self-assertions very seriously and challenges people toward a deeper engagement with these profound life questions. In the following, we will use the same sequence of contemporary spiritual issues presented in the overview above to see how each relates to and is addressed by Jesus' double question.

Spiritual Yearnings and Jesus' Double Question

- How can a free expression of self and emotions occur healthily without the safety of God's dependable love, affecting our self-perception and perception of others? According to Jesus, God is the supreme artist who loves us. In his safety, we can grow in godly imagination and can express freely on account of his safe love and transforming goodness. How can we realize our dreams and find liberation from normalcy when we have not found a way to our true self and to our Maker? A new way of self-realization in the context of God's love serves as the foundation to the true realization of dreams.
- How can the power of the satanic world be tolerated in the light of God's good and healing power? God rejects and overcomes the enemy of life, the chief liar, deceiver, murderer, and master of the culture of death.
- How is community and relationship truly realizable when participants do not know who they are and who their Maker is?

147

- How can the model of a serving, benevolent authority become a reality when leaders have not answered for themselves who they are and who their God is? How can they lead unless they are willing to be led? Jesus turns out to be the gentle leader.
- How is a true search for transcendence possible when we do not know who God really is and who we are? True self-exposure in the presence of Christ is the first step in the right direction.
- How can we truly know the cosmos when we do not know where we stand, who we are, and who the Maker of the cosmos is?[29] God gives us knowledge of the mind's purpose and proper use. He informs us, for example, that man's epistemological and scientific starting point is skewed on account of intellectual and moral autonomy and is thus in need of recalibrating restoration. C. S. Lewis once said: "Five senses; an incurably abstract intellect; a haphazardly selective memory; a set of preconceptions and assumptions so numerous that I can never examine more than a minority of them—never become conscious of them all. How much of total reality can such an apparatus let through?"[30]
- How can we determine what simplicity and spirituality are when we know neither God nor ourselves? Self-knowledge is an incentive to seek God.

Jesus' call aims at belonging first to the Creator who facilitates all else. Only then are we able to know ourselves and others.

Spiritual Self-Disclosures (Pains) and Jesus' Double Question

- How can I overcome the painful and broken separation from myself and from God? There is profound honesty in Jesus' deconstruction of his disciples. The root of all

---

29. We must be able to answer, e.g., the question of how we are meant to utilize our rational faculties, or whether our epistemological starting point is fallacious or reliable.
30. C. S. Lewis, *A Grief Observed* (New York: HarperCollins, [1961] 1989), 76.

148

existential pain is the perceived absence of God which, in turn, prohibits true knowledge of ourselves and others. Suffering and grasping at something often go hand in hand. While answering Jesus' double question does not remove suffering, it gives a place of safety in which suffering can be endured and, perhaps, even partially understood. This is because God is, loves, and transforms. C. S. Lewis aptly states: "[The Christian] does not think God will love us because we are good, but that God will make us good because He loves us."[31]

- Jesus thus gives us the courage and reason to reject the notions of fate, absolute determinism, submission to horoscopes, and New Age as soulless, mechanistic God-substitutes.

- On account of my autonomy, I am becoming my own black hole without God's intervention. God's true love wins the heart and focuses me on meaning and purpose.

Spiritual Self-Assertions (Self-Protections) and Jesus' Double Question

- How can I formulate a view of the world if my experiences and opinions do not accord with all of reality and truth? I need to be deconstructed in my intellectual (and moral) autonomy and fallibility, so that I may find the right starting point for true knowledge and meaningful morality.

- How can human rights be respected without people shouldering their respective responsibilities in the reality of this world? God's love leads to and motivates toward taking responsibility in the context of human dignity.

- How can I make sure that I perceive and approach the totality of reality (including testimonies of God's acts in history) appropriately? See the first point above.

31. C. S. Lewis, *Mere Christianity* (London: HarperCollins, [1952] 2001), 63.

- How can I persist in finding meaning without self-awareness and God-awareness? God exists, loves sacrificially, and tells us who we are.
- How can I testify to my submission to truth if I do not know myself or God? Each of us needs to be carefully deconstructed.
- How can I know anything well as long as my epistemological starting point is skewed? C. S. Lewis comments: "What you see and what you hear depends a great deal on where you are standing. It also depends on what sort of person you are."[32]
- How can I treat history appropriately when I do not know how to use my rational abilities? I need to find a true, nonreductionist philosophy of history.

Regarding those elements which Jesus rejects or challenges in contemporary spirituality, G. K. Chesterton remarks:[33]

> A man was meant to be doubtful about himself, but undoubting about the truth; this has been exactly reversed. Nowadays the part of a man that a man does assert is exactly the part he ought not to assert—himself. The part he doubts is exactly the part he ought not to doubt—the Divine Reason.

Contemporary Spiritualities Related to Jesus' Fundamental Resolution to the Double Crisis[34]

Once a representative of contemporary spiritualities earnestly addresses Jesus' searching double question of self-perception and God-perception, he or she is faced with a formidable deconstructive challenge. This challenge turns on the question of whether Jesus is right in his disarming diagnosis of human nature, seeing us as highly valued and precious and simultaneously as profoundly defaced and broken. Likewise, the existence of a personal God

32. C. S. Lewis, *The Magician's Nephew* (New York: HarperCollins, [1955] 2004), 75.
33. G. K. Chesterton, *Orthodoxy* (New York: John Lane, 1909), 31.
34. See above, pp. 81–84.

coming so close to the predicament of the human condition may unsettle or raise doubt as well.

Jesus offers a very simple yet profound three-part answer to any open-hearted person engaged in contemporary spiritualities:

- The deep problem of a defiled though highly valuable human heart cannot be resolved by the individual himself or herself.
- The human condition is known to the personal triune God.
- The healing of the broken condition, which is the consequence of a willful alienation from God as Creator, is accomplished by Jesus, the eternal and divine Son. He sacrifices himself to address the profound guilt and shame of human autonomy from God while at the same time communicating profound and healing love for any representative of contemporary spirituality.

If and when this turning occurs, a radical change ensues, which Jesus likens to nothing less than a new birth (John 3:3, 5, 8; 1 Peter 1:3) which issues in lifelong dependence upon the triune God.

Regarding spiritual yearnings, the core antidote in discipleship is that Jesus invites human beings to follow him and to be with him. All are invited to surrender to Christ, due to his gentle authority and personal love (cf. Matt. 11:28–30). Jesus, by means of the Holy Spirit, exerts a transcendent, enduring, and transforming presence which encourages imagination. (This is seen in his parables.) Jesus gives hope and surprises with true life.

Regarding spiritual self-disclosures, the core antidote in discipleship is the safety to open up and confess. Discipleship facilitates openness, due to Jesus' safe love and powerful but gentle authority. Jesus heals hypocrisy and brokenness. Jesus facilitates beneficial suffering and his people's sacrificial service in the world.

Regarding spiritual self-assertions, the core antidote in discipleship is Jesus' call to turn away from autonomy and to seek

151

renewal in God. The call to turn from intellectual or experiential autonomy and idolatry to God-dependence and to accept a universe in which there are absolutes is fundamental. Clearly, Jesus challenges this idolatrous and persistent aspect of human existence. He is the personified, incarnate truth. Therefore, radical change must happen here.

Jesus as Creator incarnate knows each culture's underlying yearnings, self-disclosures, and self-assertions better than we do. As a good physician, he offers both diagnosis and therapy. Jesus' call to discipleship reflects how God fundamentally sees our human condition and what he provides for its healing and transformation. The self-revelation of God through Jesus calls us to be healed from our persistent autonomy (idols), woundedness, and emptiness and to be restored to worship of the real and majestic God in the midst of the community of faith.

Contemporary Spiritualities and Jesus' Eight Core Character Traits

These contemporary yearnings, self-disclosures, and self-assertions are more deeply affirmed, rejected, or transformed (from a self-centered to a God-centered focus) by considering the eight core characteristics which Jesus engenders in all who follow him (see chapter 6). Jesus creates a new worshipping humanity around the central reality of God as Creator of a good universe, redeemer from alienation, and transformer of disciples into people reflecting his beauty and design.

Everyone, however, who has responded to Jesus' deconstruction and reconstruction of the human heart will need to remember that their turning to Jesus and his redeeming and restoring work leads to a permanent dependence upon him. Growing in the eight core characteristics can thus only occur in sustained, ongoing dependence upon the triune God. Furthermore, we maintain that the eight core characteristics are universal and fundamental aspects of God-facilitated and God-pleasing spirituality, lying below particular expressions of contemporary, culturally specific spirituality.

Spiritual Yearnings and Jesus' Eight Core Character Traits. Growing in the eight core characteristics in a consistent dependence upon God's love and covenant will give partial answers to contemporary spiritual yearnings. Some yearnings, such as free expression of self and feelings, growing in community and family, finding authentic leaders, finding true transcendence, discovering true understanding of the origin of the universe, and simplicity in living may be partially realized as we progress in the eight core characteristics modeled and enabled by Jesus.

For instance, community and family are facilitated by humility and forgiveness. In true surrender to God's real call, true transcendence grows. Authentic leaders will be found if they have themselves gone through the process of humbling and forgiveness.

Freedom of self-expression grows on the soil of God's purifying love and accepting ourselves as God sees us: forgiven in Christ, reconciled enemies of God in Christ's sacrifice, transformed toward godliness.

Trusting God contains many elements of adventure, as the triune God is the creator of art, innovation, and creativity.

Spiritual Self-Disclosures and Jesus' Eight Core Character Traits. Once our lives are based on the ultimate center of the universe and experience, we receive the healing and restoration we so desperately need. Many aspects expressed in our spiritual self-disclosures are addressed here.

While a life lived in the love of God expressed centrally in the work of Jesus will be transformative, growth in the eight core characteristics will not abolish the deep sense of suffering, evil, grief, isolation, and loss of meaning. However, growth in the eight core characteristics will, in time, transform us. We will gradually become humans who live in the love of God which he displays in his relentless pursuit of us. We will thus gradually be healed and freed from some forms of pain, self-absorption, and superstition. Surrender to God will gradually lead to freedom from an unhealthy focus on self.

Spiritual Self-Assertions and Jesus' Eight Core Character Traits. The central element of self-assertions is a callused or self-protective mindset, which establishes intellectual, volitional, and emotional conditions. In essence, self-assertions are idols developed out of self-protection and self-defense.

As we surrender these idols in the safety of Christ's presence, we are being transferred from keeping our unknown selves at the center of the universe to a God-centered place of being known by God. In other words, we move from idolatry to true worship of the Creator. We humbly surrender our preconceived, self-generated worldview to a God-given place and worldview. As we grow in the eight core characteristics, we bear rights and responsibilities, we learn a gentle form of exercising authority, we treat Scripture as what it claims to be. In addition, we express faith in the God of Scripture without hatred of those holding other views, we humbly seek to formulate a worldview within which science operates freely, based on trust and humility. We learn to use our rational abilities in the context of total reality, as the brokenness of those abilities is being healed. Surrender to God releases purpose, hope, and creativity, although in the midst of letting go of self-determination.

Summary. Taking contemporary expressions of spiritual yearnings, self-disclosures, and self-assertions together, we conclude: Because he is God Incarnate, the Truth, Jesus calls us to holistic worship of the triune God as the unifying core of authentic existence. Jesus transforms and matures his disciples toward God-dependent Christlikeness in character and actions. In doing so, he addresses our most fundamental existential need.

In all of this, the central issue is the heart: it drives the will, the mind, the actions, and sets parameters. Jesus says: "Where your treasure is, there your heart will be also" (Matt. 6:21). Thomas Chalmers notes: "The only way to dispossess the heart of an old affection is by the expulsive power of a new one."[35]

35. From Thomas Chalmers's sermon "The Expulsive Power of a New Affection" (n.d.). He lived from 1780–1847.

154

Conclusion

A careful analysis of spiritual yearnings, self-disclosures, and self-assertions yields much insight into the modern matrix of authentic yearnings and defacing pains on the one hand, and ill-directed self-sufficiencies (idols) on the other. Jesus' radical and necessary deconstruction and reconstruction in his call to discipleship addresses these yearnings, pains, self-protections, and idols. It serves as a meaningful answer to contemporary spiritual self-expressions in that Jesus mirrors to us the beauty and ruin of our human nature. The foundation of Christ's atonement as the resolution of the double crisis toward growth in the eight core characteristics constitutes a fundamental reversal from living autonomously. Based on Jesus' intervention, we can live and mature in a reconciled, dependent relationship with the Creator, ourselves, and others. From this basis, each disciple may then develop further into the various social and professional expressions of life.

Jesus' fundamental deconstructive and reconstructive call to discipleship offers a key to each individual's life by which to affirm, reject, and transform various expressions in contemporary cultures. The natural connection between discipleship and contemporary spirituality is surprising. Jesus' call to discipleship goes out toward healing of brokenness and a change of heart and mind. It summons us to move from idolatrous autonomy and isolation to worshipful dependence on God, issuing in a serving community and true enablement for fruitful action. To those with ears to hear, Jesus' call to discipleship offers the only real answers to the spiritual questions of life.

Conclusion

THE GOSPEL OF MARK represents a reliable ancient biographical account of the work and teaching of Jesus. It describes why Jesus has the authority to call his followers to such radical, fall-reversing discipleship.

We have seen that Jesus exposes and addresses fundamental root alienations in human existence, leading to true forgiveness from guilt, shame, and fear, giving clear purpose, and offering a stable moral orientation. In short, he ushers in the new humanity by restoring (and surpassing) the creational order.

In the call of Jesus, we are to become God-dependent (cf. Jer. 13:11):

- In our spiritual, physical, and emotional life.
- In formulating our worldview and ethical principles.
- In our approach to God's self-revelation.
- In our understanding of human nature as valuable and yet alienated and rebellious against God.
- In our daily life and work, as well as our service to others.

The fundamental self-denial as a condition to appropriating new life in Jesus should be seen as surrender of self-determination and control, not as self-abasement. The goal of self-denial is newness of life in Christ-dependence (following Christ). It is resurrection life, which means that we are progressively catching up with what is true about us in Christ. Paul puts this same truth in terms of being dead in Christ and being alive with Christ, and thus the need to put to death what opposes Christ and prayerfully finding the fruit of godliness (see Col. 3:1–17).

While Jesus begins with the transformation of the individual (although sometimes exposing an individual to a transformed community of disciples!), his outlook is always communal. Both the individual follower and the community under Christ are to reflect aspects of the character and mission of the triune God. The individual and communal core characteristics described in this study constitute new kingdom patterns. These reflect the character of the King and Messiah, and display the new and redeemed humanity in Christ. The core characteristics are not to be kept in the ghetto of the church; rather, they are to mark all areas of individual and public life in every sphere of society. Communities of Christ's followers who are being transformed by him are to be salt and light in their radical, intellectual, and personal surrender to the triune God. The call to make disciples is a consequence of becoming a disciple. Disciple-making is both reciprocal and progressive.

The result of Christ's amazing impact on receptive individuals and communities is nothing less than all-encompassing transformation, by which the Western division between knowledge and action, as well as individualism, is overcome. Christ, the eternal Son of God, rules supreme, transforms profoundly, and enables his followers to reflect core characteristics of his kingdom, to the praise of the triune God and his redeemed creation. We are thus led to worship in all areas of life, thought, and action.

> To him who loves us and has freed us from our sins by his blood and made us a kingdom, priests to his God and Father, to him be glory and dominion forever and ever. Amen. (Rev. 1:5–6)

> To him who sits on the throne and to the Lamb be blessing and honor and glory and might forever and ever! . . . And the elders fell down and worshiped. (Rev. 5:13–14)

Appendix A:
Contemporary Challenges
of—and Answers to—
the Origin and Formation
of Mark's Account

Popular Contemporary Challenges

Many popular and academic presentations on the origin of Christianity continue to view the canonical Gospels, including Mark, as early Christian constructs. These presentations see the canonical Gospels as containing considerable faith-projections around the relatively simple peasant-preacher Jesus of Nazareth. According to that ill-advised perspective, the reader of Mark is not confronted with the real historical Jesus, but rather with the belief of a particular community of the early church. Reading Mark, from this viewpoint, is essentially a study in psychology in which the reader is merely able to glance into the religious psyche of an early Christian group and its approach to life. Mark thus does not testify to historical events but to religious perceptions, hopes, and aspirations.

A much popularized version of this modern view is Dan Brown's *The Da Vinci Code*.[1] While Brown claims that he writes a novel, a good number of his statements are presented as if

1. Dan Brown, *The Da Vinci Code* (New York: Doubleday, 2003).

159

representing truth and history. Among the many false and/or misleading claims in the book, we find the following:

- "The Bible is a product of man . . . not of God. . . . Man created it as a historical record of tumultuous times and it has evolved through countless translations, additions, and revisions" (231).[2]
- "The earlier gospels [Gnostic gospels] were outlawed, gathered up, and burned" (234).[3]
- "More than eighty gospels were considered for the New Testament, and yet only a relative few were chosen for inclusion" (231).[4]
- Jesus' divinity was advanced only at the Council of Nicea (A.D. 325). Brown claims: "until that moment in history, Jesus was viewed by his followers as a mortal prophet" (233).[5]

In a misleading way, Brown thus suggests that there were multiple competing "early Christianities."[6] This postulate assumes an early Christian pluralism, which leads to a critique of the orthodox place of the canonical Gospels.

More serious and academically researched are the kindred views of such scholars as Bart Ehrman and Elaine Pagels. They have aligned themselves with the long-standing historical-critical construct[7] which claims that the faction from which the canonical Gospels arose was only one among various competing Christian groups. Orthodoxy is presented as the result of a power struggle with a Constantinian outcome. Most notably, the "proto-orthodox" faction associated with the Gospel of Mark competed with proto-

2. Against this claim, see chapter 1 above, as well as this entire appendix A.

3. See below, regarding the fact that the Gnostic Gospels were all written considerably later than the canonical Gospels.

4. See below, pages 162–63.

5. This ignores, e.g., the fact that the Gospel of Mark (ca. A.D. 65) clearly states that Jesus was condemned on charges of blasphemy for effectively claiming equality with Yahweh before the high priest.

6. Brown, *Da Vinci Code*, 242. Some of the following came to my attention through my student Lance Qualmann.

7. See especially Walter Bauer, *Orthodoxy and Heresy* (1934; Philadelphia: Fortress Books, 1979), followed, e.g., by Philipp Vielhauer, Helmut Koester, and Heikki Räisänen.

Gnostic thought which was eventually recorded in the Nag Hammadi collection (see especially the Gospel of Thomas).[8] Pagels states: "It is the winners who write history—their way. No wonder then that the viewpoint of the successful majority has dominated all traditional accounts of the origin of Christianity. . . ."[9] The basic questions remain: was it politics that did not permit Gnostic texts to be included in the canon, or did this exclusion occur because long-established, apostolically authenticated witness accounts had been around for too long prior to the rise of speculative Gnostic-Christian thought?[10]

Such views have two components. One stems from the heritage of historical-critical scholarship going back to the Enlightenment and its rationalistic view of history (immanent cause-and-effect in history). The other component contains debatable historical arguments and positions. As an example of such a dual approach, we briefly mention some of the arguments of Bart Ehrman.

Ehrman assumes the untenable and outdated posture of a "neutral" judicious observer and historian. For instance, in his preface to *The New Testament* he states: "The students are introduced . . . to other surviving pieces of early Christian literature through the early second century. . . . For example: do Mark, John, and Thomas understand the significance of Jesus in the same way?"[11] He slyly includes noncanonical texts as though they suddenly had equal rights at the table. Ignoring the historical weight and unique significance of the canonical Gospels, Ehrman then states laconically: "the Synoptic Gospels . . . are generally more useful for the task [of historical reconstruction] than the later Gospels of John, Thomas, and Peter."[12] Ehrman postulates multiple

---

8. Against Bart Ehrman see the works of Richard Bauckham, Simon Gathercole, Ben Witherington, Darrell Bock, Nicholas Perrin, and Rainer Riesner.

9. Elaine Pagels, *The Gnostic Gospels* (New York: Vintage Books, 1979), 142.

10. For a critique of the contemporary advocacy of multiple early Christianities, see Timothy P. Jones, *Misquoting Truth: A Guide to the Fallacies of Bart Ehrman's Misquoting Jesus*, 2nd ed. (InterVarsity: Downers Grove, IL, 2007).

11. Bart Ehrman, *The New Testament: A Historical Introduction to the Early Christian Writings* (New York/Oxford: Oxford University Press, 1997), preface.

12. Ibid., 196. See against Ehrman, Nicholas Perrin, *Lost in Transmission: What We Can Know about the Words of Jesus* (Nashville: Thomas Nelson, 2008), and http://ehrmanproject.com/ (accessed 1/24/2011).

expressions of "early Christianities," combined with old-fashioned and, to a degree, questionable historical-critical assumptions.[13]

To sustain a position of "multiple early Christianities," Ehrman and others have to ignore at least five central historical facts:

- The canonical Gospels predate the earliest Gnostic Gospels by some fifty years.
- The traditional authorship-identification of the four canonical Gospels has significant historical support: the authors are either identified as apostolic (Matthew and John) or associated with apostles (Mark and Luke). No such support can be found for any of the Gnostic writings.
- The canonical Gospels present Jesus in the historical context and worldview of contemporary Palestinian Judaism. In contrast, the later Gnostic Gospels are markedly ahistorical and devoid of narrative, sharing in the anti-biblical, neo-Platonic low view of the physical world. The worldview represented in the canonical Gospels and that of the Gnostic Gospels are mutually exclusive. See, e.g., the Gospel of Thomas, Logion 114c, concerning Mary: "For every woman who makes herself male will enter the kingdom of heaven."
- The core canon, consisting of the four Gospels, Acts, and ten letters of Paul, already existed around A.D. 100,[14] e.g., before the composition of the Nag Hammadi texts. Clement of Rome's letter to the Corinthians in A.D. 96 also attests to the core canon.
- Irenaeus, far from being a biased proponent of the "proto-orthodox" wing as Ehrman, Pagels, and others appear to make him out to be, was motivated in his writings against Gnostic Gospels by his knowledge of the historical prec-

13. Arguments such as: (a) even Mark is the product of the early Christian faith; (b) Jesus did not claim to be the Messiah or the Danielic Son of Man; (c) Jesus did not predict his substitutionary atonement or his resurrection.

14. See John Wenham, *Christ and the Bible* (Eugene, OR: Wipf and Stock, 2008).

edent of the canonical Gospels. It is from this vantage point that he argues against the authenticity, e.g., of the Gospel of Judas—a document which, as it now turns out, he properly represented and justifiably rejected.

Some conservative students of the Gospels may glibly dismiss these historical-critical and relativizing perspectives as liberal and believe that labeling such positions already solves the many serious questions that have been advanced against the authenticity of Mark since the Enlightenment. It is, however, insufficient to state that we no longer live in the age of modernism and thus do not need to address questions of authenticity. If historical-critical arguments concerning Mark proved historically convincing, then the postmodern or transmodern reengagement with Mark would be building a castle in the clouds. We thus propose that the serious student of the Markan text and message must address the issues of authenticity (including its textual reliability, historicity, literary character, and theological message) as well as relevance.

To leave the question of authenticity to those who undercut the authenticity of Mark, arguably on unsubstantiated grounds, means eventually to abandon the relevance of Mark's message. No study of Mark as the foundation for spiritual growth and discipleship can avoid such fundamental and far-reaching challenges posed to the Gospel by contemporary critical scholars and popular writers. It is therefore necessary to engage critically with such questions.

Modern Criticism and the Origin and Formation of Mark's Gospel Revisited

Contemporary challenges to the authenticity and relevance of Mark are but a sampling of the many questions being raised against the work. Critical voices abound regarding the historical origin of Mark, the literary character of the text, and its message.

Overview

Many modern historical-critical scholars and popular writers are convinced that Mark's Gospel arose in the early church (around A.D. 70–80), long after the recounted events. Its contents represent considerable reinterpretation of who Jesus really was (e.g., form-criticism). According to critics, the question of authorship cannot be determined.

While some scholars do admit that the most fitting literary genre for Mark is indeed that of bios (ancient biography), they quickly add that Mark belongs to a group of bios documents that apparently takes much liberty in composition and basically presents the writer's perspective rather than a faithful witness-portrait of Jesus and his disciples.

Finally, based on the assumptions of origin and literary character, the message of Mark is, according to many critical scholars and popular writers, not historically true. In their view, it represents a composite mixture of limited historical data, theological reflection upon the Old Testament, and contemporary (i.e., approximately A.D. 70) needs of the nascent Christian church. In other words, according to their view, we do not find in the Gospel of Mark Jesus and the disciples in the setting of Galilee and Judea around A.D. 30, but rather the psychological and spiritual situation among some Christians around A.D. 70. The Markan testimony, therefore, that Jesus claimed to be the Messiah, the eternal Son of God, is not reliable testimony but constitutes merely the communal belief of some early Christians. According to some critical scholars, other "Christians" around the same time perceived Jesus quite differently and in the framework of a proto-Gnostic, anti-physical redeemer expectation.

Yet recent study of the Gospel of Mark has yielded considerable alternatives to these critical views. As noted above, these views stem from a combination of Enlightenment presuppositions and the questionable handling of historical, literary, and theological evidence. Seemingly settled issues have been reopened and reevaluated in recent decades.

164

Among these are:

- A renewed appreciation for the fact that Mark uses the ancient genre of bios in a conservative and careful way (see chapter 1).
- An in-depth understanding of Jesus' use of pedagogy common in contemporary synagogues and homes, shedding light on the memorization and learning process which Jesus undertook with his disciples, thus guaranteeing true witness rather than permitting faith-projections (see also chapter 1).
- A historically relevant reevaluation of messianic expectations at the time of Jesus and their correspondence to an inner-Markan tension between popular messianic expectations and Jesus' own messianic self-revelation (see chapter 4).
- A historically relevant reevaluation of the popular expectation in Palestinian Judaism of the kingdom of God versus Jesus' own teaching on the subject (see chapters 3 and 4).

These topics have been examined in some detail in the preceding chapters. Three other significant issues remain to be addressed.

A Sober Assessment of the Date of Mark

External and Internal Evidence. Especially due to Papias, other early Fathers, and various other early manuscripts, as well as internal evidence from the Gospel itself, Mark is most convincingly dated around A.D. 65. None of the arguments assuming that the author of Mark looks back at the destruction of Jerusalem and the temple (A.D. 70) are convincing. It is possible, however, that the persecution of Christians under Nero (A.D. 64) had already occurred prior to the composition of Mark.[15]

15. See, e.g., Martin Hengel, "The Gospel of Mark: Time of Origin and Situation," in Hengel, *Studies in the Gospel of Mark* (Philadelphia: Fortress, 1985), 1–30.

Patristic evidence concerning the existence of the Gospel is abundant. Irenaeus (A.D. 180), for example, speaks of a "fourfold gospel."[16] He cites Mark 1:24; 5:31, 41, 43; 8:31, 38; 9:23, 44–45; 10:38; 13:32, as well as 16:19.[17] Also, Tatian's *Diatessaron* (~A.D. 160) assumes the existence of the Gospel of Mark. Prior to Irenaeus and Tatian perhaps the Shepherd of Hermas (~A.D. 140) and Justin Martyr (~A.D. 150, *Dialogue with Trypho*[18]) may point to the existence of Mark. Papias (~A.D. 110–20) knows of Mark as composer of the Gospel.[19] Among other early Apostolic Fathers, Mark is rarely mentioned. Only Clement of Rome may be referring to Mark 7:6 and 6:34.[20]

Additionally, Patristic evidence for the time of Mark's composition is convincing. Clement of Alexandria,[21] Jerome,[22] and Origen[23] state that Mark wrote his Gospel while Peter was still alive.[24] If this is so, Mark would have to have been written prior to A.D. 64–66, assuming Clement of Rome is correctly interpreted to be speaking of the double martyrdom of Peter and Paul around that time. On the other hand, the Anti-Marcionite Gospel Prologue[25] (~A.D. 160–80) holds the view that Mark as the translator of Peter composed his Gospel in Italy (Rome) following Peter's death. Papias may not be used as an arbitrator between the two contrasting patristic positions, although it is slightly more likely that Papias implies the composition of Mark during the lifetime of Peter.

16. Irenaeus, *Adv. Haer.*, 3.11.8.
17. Ibid., 3.10.6.
18. Compare, e.g., *Dialogue with Trypho*, 88, with Mark 6:3 and 12:30: Justin refers to Jesus as a carpenter/builder, a term which only Mark 6:3/12:30 uses (not in Matt. 13:55 or Luke 4:22).
19. See Bo Reicke, *The Roots of the Synoptic Gospels* (Minneapolis: Fortress Press, 1986), ad loc.
20. See the "Markan style" in 1 Clement 15:2, 4, 7. Compare 1 Clement 24:5 with Mark 4:3; 1 Clement 46:8 with Mark 14:21 and 9:42; 1 Clement 15:2 with Mark 7:6.
21. Eusebius, *Hist. eccl.* 6.14.6–7.
22. Jerome, *De Vir*, 3.8.
23. See Eusebius, *Hist. eccl.* 6.25.5.
24. Eusebius relies upon Papias, who in turn reports as a direct witness for the presbyter and apostle John.
25. Which, at times, contains less widely held views (see, e.g., the Shepherd of Hermas).

Thus the preponderance of the external evidence points to the fact that the Gospel of Mark is widely known in Asia Minor and Italy at least by A.D. 100, if not earlier.

Internal evidence from the Gospel itself also supports a date of composition of around A.D. 65.

Rudolf Pesch[26] represents many scholars who are convinced that Mark 13 presupposes the events of the Jewish War (A.D. 66–70) and the destruction of the Jerusalem temple in A.D. 70. This position, however, has been substantially challenged by J. A. T. Robinson.[27] The evidence in favor of dating Mark after the destruction of Jerusalem and the temple is tentative at best.

The reference to consecrated bread in Mark 2:26 may imply the present (i.e., at the time of Mark's writing) continuity of the temple tradition, especially the general statement: "which is lawful only for the priests to eat" (2:26). It is well known that a few post–A.D. 70 writings speak of the temple system in generic terms.[28] However, these documents simply show that writers did at times refer to the truth of the temple system after it ceased without referring to its present practice. The question regarding Mark 2:26 is thus to be considered on its own merit.

Wenham[29] suggests that after Peter escaped from prison in A.D. 42, he preached to the Jews in Rome, while Mark commits some of Peter's preaching to writing in the form of the Gospel.

Based on all available data, we conclude that external and internal evidence most convincingly leads to dating Mark at around A.D. 65.

Gnostic Gospels. As for the Gnostic Gospels, it is historically responsible to maintain that such books as the Gospel of Thomas are most likely dependent on the earliest Christian canonical

26. Rudolf Pesch, *Das Markusevangelium*, 3rd ed. (Freiburg: Herder, 1980), 1:14.
27. J. A. T. Robinson, *Redating the New Testament* (Louisville: Westminster John Knox, 1977), ad loc.
28. See esp. Josephus, *Ant.* 3.151 and 1 Clement 40, 5– 41, 2.
29. John Wenham, *Redating Matthew, Mark, and Luke: A Fresh Assault on the Synoptic Problem* (London: Hodder & Stoughton, 1991), 146–72.

writings and should all be dated some 50 years after the canonical Gospels.[30]

Recent study by Rudolf Schnackenburg[31] (and others) has shown that even the Gospel of John is not connected with proto-Gnostic or Gnostic thought, but rather reflects widespread forms of contrasting expressions which are also found, e.g., at the Jewish community of Qumran. In contrast to John, there is no question that the Gospel of Thomas, the Gospel of Mary, the Gospel of Peter, and the Gospel of Judas are Gnostic in tone.

Beyond Schnackenburg's detailed discussion, Evans has presented convincing arguments in support of the historical primacy and originality of the canonical Gospels. In a lengthy excursus[32] Evans interacts with the analyses of Bertil Gärtner, Robert Grant, Ernst Haenchen, John Meier, Wolfgang Schrage, Klyne Snodgrass, Christopher Tuckett, and others. He comes to the convincing conclusion that none of the apocryphal Gospels (such as the Gospel of Thomas, Egerton 2, the Gospel of the Hebrews, the Secret Gospel of Mark, or the Gospel of Peter) preceded or predated the Synoptic canonical Gospels.[33]

A Renewed Appreciation of Early Patristic Information regarding Mark's Author

More significant even than the question of the date of Mark is the question of its author. If the author can be identified as a personal companion of Paul and especially of Peter, then it follows that the content of Mark is directly connected with apostolic witness and exposed to apostolic verification or falsification. In other words, if there is a convergence of a relatively early date *and* Markan authorship, it means that the Gospel was written at a time during which living apostles and eyewitnesses were

30. For good discussion concerning the Gospel of Thomas, see Nicholas Perrin, *Thomas: The Other Gospel* (Louisville: Westminster John Knox, 2007).

31. Rudolf Schnackenburg, *The Gospel According to St. John*, Herder's Theological Commentary on the New Testament (New York: Herder and Crossroad, 1987), 1:135–52.

32. Craig Evans, *Mark 8:27–16:20*, Word Biblical Commentary 34b (Nashville: Nelson, 2001), xxx–xliii; see the extensive literature on pp. xxx–xxxii.

33. Ibid., xlii–xliii.

able to affirm or question its content. In this regard, the Papias fragment (A.D. 120) is of particular significance, as Papias clearly states that John Mark, a relative of the Levite (Joseph) Barnabas from Cyprus (Acts 4:36; Col. 4:10) is the companion of Peter who wrote down what Peter said about Jesus.

Widespread patristic evidence[34] affirms this tradition that Mark was the *hermeneutes* of Peter.[35] But it has been held in historical-critical circles for many decades that we simply do not know who wrote the Gospel of Mark. It is true that the heading "According to Mark" was added later to the Gospel.[36] Technically speaking, the second Gospel is thus an anonymous work. To deny any knowledge about authorship based on this fact alone means, however, to ignore significant and ancient external and internal evidence in support of Markan authorship.

External Evidence for Markan Authorship. As stated above, a decisive group of patristic authors considers John Mark to be the writer of the second Gospel as well as the companion of Peter.[37] Only Hippolytus (~A.D. 200) differentiates between the cousin of Barnabas (John Mark) and a certain evangelist Mark, author of the Gospel.

Of particular significance are the brief extant statements by Papias, Bishop of Hierapolis (~A.D. 110–20), preserved by Eusebius of Caesarea (A.D. 260–340). Papias[38] states that he received oral

34. See, for example, Justin Martyr, Irenaeus, Clement of Alexandria, Tertullian, Origen, and Jerome.

35. Eusebius, *Hist. eccl.* 3.39.15. It is less likely that "*hermeneutes*" denotes "translator" from one language to another; rather, Mark wrote down what he heard from Peter, according to his (or Peter's?) memory. Mark could not be termed an amanuensis, since Peter apparently did not dictate the Gospel to Mark. See the excellent discussion of recent research on Papias in Rainer Riesner, "Die Rückkehr der Augenzeugen," *Theologische Beiträge*, 38 (2007): 337–52, esp. 342–44, with particular reference to Richard Bauckham, *Jesus and the Eyewitnesses: The Gospels as Eyewitness Testimony* (Grand Rapids: Eerdmans, 2006).

36. At the latest at the end of the second century A.D. Concerning an earlier date, see Martin Hengel, "The Titles of the Gospels and the Gospel of Mark," in *Studies in the Gospel of Mark* (Philadelphia: Fortress, 1985), 64–84.

37. Cf. Pesch, *Das Markusevangelium*, 1:4–11 on an extensive discussion of this issue, as well as the aforementioned Papias, Irenaeus, Clement of Alexandria, Origen, and Jerome.

38. Eusebius, *Hist. eccl.* 3.39.1–7.14–17. See Robert Yarbrough, "The Date of Papias: A Reassessment," *JETS* 26, 2 (June 1983): 181–91, and C. Clifton Black, *Mark: Images of an Apostolic Interpreter* (Columbia: University of South Carolina, 1994).

tradition from the presbyter and apostle John.[39] Concerning the Gospel of Mark, Papias states that Mark was the writer for Peter; that he wrote down accurately as much as he could remember of Peter's words, which the latter had adapted to the needs of the moment; that he did not write in a particular order[40] what the Lord said and did (according to Papias, however, the lack of precise chronological order vouches for the Gospel's authenticity as stemming from Peter and thus confirms the Gospel of Mark as a reliable apostolic document); that he was not an eyewitness or disciple of Jesus; and that he did not intend to omit or misrepresent anything. According to Papias, the Gospel of Mark gains its apostolic and reliable character on account of these factors.

What appears to cast doubt on the independent value of his report is the fact that Papias also refers to 1 Peter 5:13.[41] This means for Pesch[42] and others that Papias must be exclusively dependent on New Testament documents for his (thus conjectured) information on Mark. While there is little doubt that Papias knew 1 Peter 5:13, this by no means justifies the assumption, especially in the light of his expressly stated case to the contrary, that he had no separate access to oral information concerning the authorship of Mark. Indeed Papias himself seems to consider succinct oral information drawn from authentic sources (here from the presbyter and apostle John) to be more

---

39. Eusebius, *Hist. eccl.* 3.29.15. It is very likely that the apostle John is also the presbyter mentioned by Papias, who refers to the (twelve) apostles as "Presbyters" (cf. Eusebius, *Hist. eccl.* 3.39.4). Identifying the "apostle John" as the "presbyter John" is plausible as both are mentioned in one phrase (Eusebius, *Hist. eccl.* 3.39.4), and especially since Papias states there that the "presbyter John" was a "disciple" of the Lord. Papias's reference to the otherwise unknown "disciple" Aristion is awkward but does not falsify the above statements. Irenaeus (*Adv. Haer.* 5.32) also supports the identification of John as "apostle" and "presbyter."

40. Cf. Justin Martyr, *Dialogue with Trypho*, 106.3. See further Irenaeus (*Adv. Haer.* 3.1.2) and Tertullian (A.D. 160–222; *Adv. Marcion* 4.5) concerning the fact that Peter is the main source of the Gospel of Mark. Walter Dickson, *Hastings Dictionary*, vol. 3 (Edinburgh: T. & T. Clark, 1909), 257, states: "The tradition is so ancient, so consistent in its main affirmations, and so widely extended, that only internal considerations of exceptional weight could justify its rejection."

41. Eusebius, *Hist. eccl.* 3.39.17.

42. Pesch, *Das Markusevangelium*, 1:4.

significant than wordy written documentation. We may not so easily rob Papias of his ostensible access to extra-biblical oral information, especially since his testimony is congruent with other patristic witnesses.

A further point of criticism against the validity of Papias's statements is that he appears to speak apologetically in favor of Mark. First it must be noted that the apologetic aim does not pertain to Mark as author[43] but rather to the content of his report. Furthermore, Papias's apologetic by no means automatically speaks against the credibility of what he affirms. Apologetic can speak for truth to offset denial or error, or it may cover up truth. Therefore, none of the arguments presented against the validity of Papias's statements stand up to scrutiny.

Patristic evidence thus makes a strong case for Mark to have written the Gospel and for Peter to be primarily responsible for its contents.

Internal Evidence for Peter as the Oral Source for Mark. Some internal indicators support the patristic testimony that Peter stands behind Mark's Gospel. In general terms, the Markan account (a) is especially vivid when recounting incidents involving Peter, (b) presents certain features of Peter's weakness, and (c) omits at times praiseworthy or noticeable references to Peter as reported in Matthew and Luke.

Regarding (a): Raymond Brown[44] is correct in observing that Peter is the unquestioned leader in earliest Palestinian Christianity, thus making a particular proximity of Mark to Peter rather difficult to prove. But in Mark's vivid report, Peter occupies a significant and central place that goes beyond that which Matthew and Luke report.[45] We emphasize the following: Mark 1:14–20 (calling of disciples); Mark 1:29 (Jesus in the house of Peter and

43. This is significant, considering the fact that Mark was not an apostle and eyewitness.

44. Raymond Brown, *An Introduction to the New Testament* (New York: Doubleday, 1997), 159.

45. See the synoptic parallels to Mark 1:36; 5:37; 8:29 (confession); 9:2 (transfiguration); 11:21; 13:3; 14:33.

171

Andrew); Mark 5:21 (Jairus's daughter); Mark 14:54, 72 (Jesus and Peter); Mark 16:7 (report concerning Jesus' resurrection). In each instance, Peter is the central figure. Furthermore, the directness of an eyewitness report is especially noticeable in Mark 1:16–20; 1:29; 5:21ff.; 9:2ff.; 14:33ff.; 14:54, 72.

Regarding (b): We note telling, (self-?) critical features in Mark 8:33; 9:5; 14:30–31; 14:66ff.

Regarding (c): It is significant that various praiseworthy or noticeable references to Peter are conspicuously missing in the Markan account. These include: (1) the report of Peter walking on water (6:45–52; contrast with Matthew 14:28–29); (2) the pericope concerning temple tax, in which Peter figures prominently (Matt. 17:24–27); (3) Jesus' prayer for Peter in Gethsemane (Luke 22:31–32); (4) Peter and the rock (Matt. 16:18). Occasionally, Peter is not mentioned by name in Mark, when Matthew and/or Luke do so.[46] Even Mark 14:13, 72 may be understood as portraying modesty or even shame by an eyewitness: Mark 14:72 omits the Matthean and Lukan remark that Peter cried "bitterly."[47] The tendency is clear: where Peter occupies a praiseworthy or prominent position, Mark's account is more muted than Matthew's or Luke's.

It has also been observed that there exists a certain structural proximity between Peter's Caesarea speech (Acts 10:34–43) and the Gospel of Mark.[48] The historical sequence of John the Baptist's circumstances, Jesus' baptism, his Galilean healing and teaching ministry, and his death and resurrection, may thus point to the fact that Peter is the originator of a simple "gospel" outline and format.

While the internal evidence is at best corroborative in nature, we note that there is an unforced and consistent convergence between patristic evidence (John Mark, author of the second Gospel, companion of Peter), and internal indicators in Mark insofar as Peter is a likely authority behind the Markan account. We now turn to the question of who John Mark was.

46. Compare, e.g., Mark 7:17 with Matthew 15:15, as well as Mark 14:13 with Luke 22:8.
47. Contrast with Matthew 26:75 and Luke 22:62.
48. See the discussion about John Mark in the following sections.

Who Was John Mark? Mark's typical formulations and syntactical constructions suggest the Hellenized, Palestinian language milieu in which the author was at home.[49] While some of the literary features display a close proximity to the Semitic language milieu, the Gospel was probably written in Greek from the outset. Hengel[50] is convinced that the author is a Greek-speaking Jewish Christian who is also familiar with Aramaic.

While patristic evidence links (John) Mark with Peter (see above), the New Testament evidence primarily portrays John Mark as a companion of Paul. The New Testament mentions Mark (or John or John Mark) nine times.[51] In Acts, John Mark frequents the house of his mother Mary in Jerusalem (Acts 12:12; prior to A.D. 46), a place at which Peter stayed as well (Acts 12:25; 13:5, 13; 15:37–39).

During the initial phase of Paul's first missionary journey (after A.D. 46), John Mark joins Barnabas and Paul (Acts 13:5; see 12:25) but deserts them in Perga, Pamphylia (Acts 13:13). Around A.D. 49–50, at the beginning of Paul's second missionary journey, John Mark is excluded from joining Paul again (Acts 13:36–39). John Mark subsequently engages in missionary work with Barnabas on Cyprus (Acts 15:39). Around A.D. 61 (see Col. 4:10; Philem. 24), John Mark is found once more in the company of Paul and as a missionary in Asia Minor.

Only around A.D. 63 is John Mark once more in Peter's company (1 Peter 5:13) in Rome. Around A.D. 64 John Mark may be in Ephesus (2 Tim. 4:11, joins Timothy to see Paul in Rome). Besides his association with Paul, John Mark appears most frequently in the company of Demas and Luke (cf. Philem. 24; 2 Tim. 4:11–12; Col. 4:7ff.).

What can account for this apparent tension between patristic/Markan evidence on the one hand (John Mark as associate of

---

49. See esp. Vincent Taylor, *The Gospel According to St. Mark: The Greek Text with Introduction, Notes, and Indexes* (New York: Macmillan, 1952), 45ff.

50. Hengel, *Studies in the Gospel of Mark*, 46.

51. Acts 12:12 (John Mark), 25 (John Mark); 13:5 (John), 13 (John); 15:37 (John Mark), 39 (Mark); 1 Peter 5:13 ("my son" Mark); Philem. 24 (Mark); Col. 4:10 (Mark, cousin of Barnabas); 2 Tim. 4:11 (Mark, useful in service). It is unlikely to posit one Mark for Papias and the Gospel of Mark, and another for Acts and the Epistles.

Peter) and much of the New Testament evidence on the other (John Mark primarily as an associate of Paul)?

First, we must note that Peter is not frequently mentioned in the New Testament subsequent to the Jerusalem Council (A.D. 49). We therefore should not expect many New Testament references to John Mark meeting Peter after A.D. 49 due to the fact that Acts 13–28 focuses on Paul the Pauline letters (see also the Pauline letters). These chapters also display a Pauline perspective with regard to the names of associates.

Second, it is highly probable that John Mark frequently met Peter in Jerusalem (A.D. 35–45) and that he maintained an (at times stormy) association with Paul from A.D. 46 to about 64.

The primary problem (contrast 1 Peter 5:13 with 2 Tim. 4:11) is, according to patristic evidence, the time John Mark spent with Peter around A.D. 62–64, prior to Peter's martyrdom. As we will suggest below, it is conceivable that, at that stage, John Mark met Peter again while continuing his association with Paul. The main bridge between John Mark, Peter, and Paul is John Mark's relative Barnabas, who brings Paul into the Jerusalem circle in the first place. In order to seek a solution to the apparent tension, two facts will prove helpful.

In the first place, it is instructive to note that the above-mentioned "double association" is not without historical parallel: Silas/Silvanus was associated with Peter and Paul in a similar way.[52] Silas is a leading disciple (Acts 15:22, 32), a Roman citizen (Acts 16:37–38), and Paul's attendant (Acts 15:40; 1 Thess. 1:1; 2 Thess. 1:1; 2 Cor. 1:19). On the other hand, he is also a companion of Peter (1 Peter 5:12). This parallel supports the view that a somewhat "untidy" historical reconstruction is closer to the truth than a one-sided, simple, and smooth explanation concerning John Mark's associations either with Peter or Paul.

In addition, according to Acts 13:5, John Mark was known as an "assistant." Some believe that this term represents the title of

52. Silas is also known as Silvanus: compare 2 Cor. 1:19 (Silvanus and Timothy) with Acts 17:14 and 18:5 (Silas and Timothy). Note even the association between Silas/Silvanus and John Mark in 1 Peter 5:12–13.

a synagogue attendant.[53] It is, however, more likely that the term refers to the fact that John Mark was at Paul's and Barnabas's disposal for service (perhaps as a secretary). Both John Mark and Silas functioned as attendants to the apostles (compare Acts 13:5 with Acts 15:40), a fact which further supports the possibility of dual association (see 2 Tim. 4:11).

It is historically plausible that John Mark began his early Christian years in the company of Peter; later he accompanied Paul and experienced temporary tension with him; toward the end of Paul's life, Mark was restored to Paul and, simultaneously, served as the assistant of Peter in Rome. The following chart illustrates a likely itinerary of John Mark.

- A.D. 44: In Jerusalem with his mother Mary; contact with Peter & Barnabas (Acts 12:12).
- A.D. 45: Goes with Paul and Barnabas to Syrian Antioch (Acts 12:25).
- A.D. 46: Joins Barnabas and Paul on Paul's first missionary journey (Acts 13:5).
- A.D. 46: Departs from Barnabas and Paul and returns to Jerusalem (Acts 13:13).
- ~A.D. 47/48: Double problem with Barnabas concerning Peter and John Mark (Acts 15:37ff.; Gal. 2).
- A.D. 49: Barnabas and John Mark travel to Cyprus following the "Antiochene conflict."
- A.D. 61: John Mark accompanies Paul to Rome/missionary in Asia Minor(?) (Philem. 23–24; Col. 4:10).
- A.D. 63?: Attendant of Peter in Rome (from "Babylon," 1 Peter 5:13).
- A.D. 64: Attendant of Paul; John Mark's sojourn in Ephesus(?) (2 Tim. 4:11).

John Mark as Witness to the Apostles. As a relative of Barnabas, John Mark grew up in the setting of Hellenistic Judaism. Through

---

53. See Luke 4:20. However, note 2 Tim. 4:11, where John Mark is identified as a useful servant.

Barnabas, he was intimately acquainted with the apostles Peter and Paul and their teaching (cf. Acts 4:36–7 and 9:26). Accompanying Paul and Barnabas, John Mark must have been the witness of many sermons both to Jews and Gentiles. Adolf Schlatter aptly states:

> Mark thus held from the beginning a central place in the church. He witnessed how the Jewish and Greek churches took shape; he enjoyed extended times of personal contact both with Peter and Paul, and thus became a special witness to the Apostolic preaching. Furthermore, he himself engaged in an extensive teaching ministry in the church.[54]

John Mark as Eyewitness of Jesus? There is a possibility that Mark was an eyewitness of events described at the end of the Gospel of Mark. Mark 14:51–52 may be a personal reminiscence inserted by the author. Certainly, the omission of these two verses would facilitate narrative continuity. Also, the detail in Mark 15:21 ("Simon of Cyrene . . . father of Alexander and Rufus"[55]) may reflect personal eyewitness reporting.[56] However, patristic evidence is divided on this question: Papias[57] speaks against Mark as an eyewitness of Jesus, while the later Muratorian Canon (~A.D. 200)[58] identifies John Mark as an eyewitness. Papias may be seen as simply defending the correct view that John Mark was neither a disciple nor a witness of the life of Christ. This does not necessarily preclude that John Mark may have become a personal witness at the end of Jesus' life.[59]

---

54. Adolf Schlatter, *Einleitung in die Bibel* (Stuttgart: Calwer, 1923), 293 (English transl., Hans F. Bayer).

55. Rufus has been identified with Rufus in Rom. 16:13, a hint that Mark is writing from Rome to Roman Christians? Not too much should be made of this possibility.

56. See also Mark 15:39.

57. Eusebius, *Hist. eccl.* 3.39.

58. See, e.g., Edgar Hennecke, *Neutestamentliche Apokryphen*, vol. 1 (Tübingen: J. C. B. Mohr/Paul Siebeck, 1968), 19. That Mark (second Gospel) is in view in this incomplete fragment may be inferred by the next line, which speaks of the "third Gospel" as that of Luke.

59. Later patristic tradition has Peter send John Mark to Egypt as a missionary where he plants the church in Alexandria and becomes its first bishop. John Mark is said to have met martyrdom in Alexandria in A.D. 68. His remains are said to have been transferred to Venice.

Regardless of this issue, we conclude that John Mark had direct access to the eyewitness Peter, leader of early Christian disciples, who was explicitly called to testify to the real Jesus and his teaching. There is thus a direct continuity of transmission from Jesus to Peter to John Mark. Jesus guarantees that Peter learns; Peter guarantees that John Mark records his teaching.

A Historically Tenable Reconstruction of the Origin and Formation of the Gospel of Mark

The formation of the written Gospel of Mark may have occurred in the following manner.

(1) It is historically plausible to assume a pre-Easter oral (and to some degree written)[60] phase of stereotyped memorization of large amounts of Jesus' teaching, including forms of *mašhal* and dialogues, as well as Jesus' deeds. This large body of memorized sayings and events was further embedded in memory by repetition. It is possible that this phase of retention and transmission occurred both in Aramaic and in Greek. A strong fidelity to that which was taught assures even in an oral (bilingual) phase the preservation of Jesus' teaching, thus partially explaining the close proximity in Greek wording among the Synoptic Gospels. Since Jesus had called a group of disciples, there was also the guarantee of mutual correction and assistance in remembering.[61]

(2) Those whom Jesus taught in a systematic way are precisely the apostolic witnesses following Jesus' death and resurrection. There is thus the phenomenon of continuity of persons involved. This assures continuity of transmission of the stereotyped body of

60. Cf. Paul Barnett, *Jesus and the Rise of Early Christianity: A History of New Testament Times* (Downers Grove, IL: InterVarsity, 1999), 40, and Carsten Thiede and Matthew D'Ancona, *Eyewitness to Jesus* (London: Doubleday, 1996), on the possibility that Matthew was capable of some form of shorthand note-taking even during the ministry of Jesus. See Brown, *An Introduction to the New Testament*, 151 and n66, regarding the combined orality and textuality in the Greco-Roman world.

61. See furthermore the fact that the risen Jesus instructs his disciples (Luke 24) and that he promised the assistance of the Holy Spirit in the process of remembering (see John 14:26 and 16:12–15). This fact serves as a significant link between the historical reconstruction and the inspiration and canonization of the Gospels as part of the written Word of God.

memorized material. Careful handling of learned contents marks the phase between Jesus and the composition of the canonical Gospels (cf., e.g., Acts 10:34–43; 20:35; 1 Cor. 11:23–25; 15:1–3).[62]

(3) While Jesus taught with prophetic and divine authority already during his public ministry, now that the messenger had been vindicated from death in such an unparalleled, unexpected, and overwhelming manner, every word and deed of the Master would be of utmost significance. The God of Abraham, Isaac, and Jacob fully vouchsafed the totality of Jesus' claims by raising him from the dead. After all, the words and deeds of the Master did not only pertain to the present will of God but also to eternal life. Furthermore, Jesus had identified himself as the future judge of humankind (Mark 8:34–38).

(4) It stands to reason that in the initial post-Easter phase the most recent events (which are even more without analogy than the rest of Jesus' life) were narrated first to those who found faith in Jesus on account of the apostles' preaching (cf. Acts 2:42; oral passion and resurrection account). Subsequently, previously memorized, preached, and experienced teaching[63] and deeds of Jesus would be catechetically (orally) combined with the recently narrated passion and resurrection account. Pesch (based on Martin Kähler)[64] thus sees Mark's Gospel as a reflection of the early post-Easter testimony (cf. Acts 10 with structure of Mark). Especially Kähler speaks of a passion account, which has been "expanded towards the beginning"[65] and considers this to be the origin of the particular outline of Mark. This view gains support from the above-mentioned fact that the proclamation about Jesus in the first Petrine sermon addressing Gentile, God-fearing people

---

62. Cf. Earle Ellis, "Preformed Traditions and Their Implications for Pauline Christology," in *Christology, Controversy and Community*, ed. David Horrell and Christopher Mark Tuckett (Leiden: Brill, 2000), 303–20, esp. 310. See Bauckham, *Jesus and the Eyewitnesses*, chapters 11 and 13.

63. Note the particularly high degree of agreement (some 80 percent) among the Synoptic Gospels with regard to Jesus' words.

64. Pesch, *Das Markusevangelium*, 1:67, and n2. M. Kähler, *Der sogenannte historische Jesus und der geschichtliche, biblische Christus*, 2nd ed. (Leipzig: A. Deichert'sche Verlagsbuchhandlung, 1896), 80n1.

65. Pesch, *Das Markusevangelium*, 1:1–40, 67, and 2:1–27. Kähler, *Der sogenannte historische Jesus*, 80n1.

in Acts (Acts 10:36–43; cf. also Acts 2:22–36; Acts 3:11–26) displays a structure similar to the Gospel of Mark.

Acts	Mark
10:34	1:1
10:37–38a	1:2–11
10:38b	1:12–9:50
10:39a	10:1–15:20
10:39b	15:21–47
10:40	16:1–8; cf. Mark 9:9
10:41	cf. Mark 9:9; Luke 24:36–43
10:42	cf. Mark 8:38; Matt. 28:19–20; Acts 1:8
10:43	cf. Mark 10:45; Luke 24:44–49; Acts 1:8

Greek and Aramaic are the most likely languages spoken during this phase. Furthermore, this witness account is cast in the genre of ancient biography (bios).

The historical probability of a passion account with a substantial "extended introduction" (orally transmitted) explains a common pattern of the Synoptic Gospel accounts. This allows for the possibility that Mark, Matthew, and Luke composed their respective Gospels independently from one another, yet were dependent on the common, stereotyped (and large) oral Gospel memory deposited especially in the minds of the apostles as well as a common outline. The length and depth of Jesus' ministry necessitates selection of—and focus on—his salient events and teachings (John 21:25).

(5) Communities of believers sprang up in Judea, Samaria, Galilee, and Syria. This called for further apostolic witness and eventually the literary fixation of the learned testimonies.

(6) It must be kept in mind that the best interpretation of Luke's prologue (Luke 1:1–4) is that while Luke was aware of different written accounts of Jesus' deeds and words, he did not use them (including Matthew, John, or Mark)[66] for his own work.

66. Frederic Godet, *Luke* (New York: Funk, 1881), 35.

Rather, he consulted Apostolic eyewitnesses[67] (perhaps even Peter [Mark?], and John). The reconstruction sketched above in the framework of a modified tradition hypothesis would thus dovetail well with Luke's prologue.

(7) Finally, Bo Reicke[68] submits the likelihood that Matthew and Mark (via Peter) as well as Mark and Luke (via Paul)[69] may have had personal contact with each other. Reicke thinks that some verbal agreements between Matthew/Mark and Mark/Luke may stem from such personal contact.[70]

Conclusion

Contrary to models of purely literary reconstructions, the historical circumstances in which the Gospel of Mark came into being suggest a strong historical link between the pre-Easter Jesus, the stable transmission of the oral apostolic eyewitness testimony, John Mark as the writer for Peter, and the written account of Mark around A.D. 65.

67. See the very informative overview of recent research on New Testament eyewitnesses by Rainer Riesner, "Die Rückkehr der Augenzeugen: Eine neue Entwicklung in der Evangelienforschung," *Theologische Beiträge* 38 (2007): 337–52.

68. Bo Reicke, *Roots of the Synoptic Gospels*, 180ff.

69. See Col. 4:10, 14; 2 Tim. 4:11; Philem. 24; John Mark and Luke were probably together during Paul's imprisonment in Caesarea.

70. The personal contact between Matthew and Luke is most difficult to prove historically.

Appendix B:
The Message of Mark 8:34
and Dietrich Bonhoeffer's
The Cost of Discipleship

The Meaning of "Carry Your Cross"

The meaning of Mark 8:34 becomes particularly clear when we grasp the historical significance of the phrase "carry your cross." When Jesus uses this phrase, he does not mean: "You must feel as miserable as possible." The significance of the phrase is much more radical than that.

The cruel Roman form of execution by crucifixion was adopted from Persia. It was the most horrifying form of punishment, used as a public deterrent to all those who would want to deviate from the imposed law and so-called pax Romana (peace of Rome) of the Roman Empire. Among Romans, "to carry your cross" was considered a great shame. The Roman author Cicero says about crucifixion: "For a Roman even to think or to name 'crucifixion' is utterly shameful."[1] But, as a deterrent, thousands of people were crucified around the time of Christ.

In preparation for crucifixion, the vertical beam of the cross was often lowered into the ground beforehand. After a person had been convicted and condemned by a Roman court, he was to carry the *patibulum*, the horizontal bar of the cross through

1. Cicero, *Servitutis extremum summumque supplicium*, in *Contra Verres* 2.5.169. See David Chapman, *Ancient Jewish and Christian Perceptions of Crucifixion* (Tübingen: Mohr Siebeck, 2008).

the streets in shame to the public place of execution, which, according to Roman and Jewish law, always had to be outside the city. The phrase "carrying your cross" was thus quite well known to everyone—Jew or Gentile, of Roman or of Hellenistic heritage—who would have heard Jesus teach. All would have been very familiar with crucifixion as a form of execution.

Most likely, then, Jesus calls his disciples to carry, figuratively speaking, their own *patibulum*, thereby causing them to realize that their lives are no longer their own. The serious and sobering implication of Jesus' teaching and his death on our behalf is that we deserve death before the justice of God, a death in which we should meet God's righteous judgment of our rebellious, autonomous unrighteousness before him and with each other—yet Jesus bore that burden for us instead. An old rabbinic interpretation of Abraham's near-sacrifice of Isaac says (Bereshith Rabba, Paragr. 56 [on Gen 22:6]): "Abraham took the wood of the offering as one who bears his cross upon his shoulders."[2]

I believe this is what Jesus means by his injunction to "carry your cross." You are no longer your own. As such, you might also have to die as one of the consequences of such surrender. The key idea is that somebody else has redeemed your life. The righteous wrath of God has been satisfied by someone who loves you deeply and sacrificially. You get to live and grow in the received righteousness of (from) God (2 Cor. 5:21; Phil. 3:9–10; see Col. 3:1–17). He will not reject you, because someone else satisfied God's wrath.

The Meaning of "Denying Yourself"

A second challenge to understanding Mark 8:34 lies in a proper explanation of the meaning of "denying yourself." I suggest that Jesus' call to "deny" ourselves includes not only to love God and others (Mark 12:30–31; Phil. 2:1–4), but also to love ourselves

---

2. Quoted in Willoughby Allen, *Matthew* (Edinburgh: T&T Clark, 1907), 111. See Adolf Schlatter, *Der Evangelist Matthäus* (Stuttgart: Calwer, 1957), 351, regarding "carry your cross" (Matt. 10:38), as well as 519–20 regarding "self-denial" (Matt. 16:24).

in the process of self-denial (Mark 12:31). In order to understand this, we must briefly consider Mark 8:35–37.

Mark 8:35 continues the foundational call to letting go and to surrender. Jesus is speaking about gaining (keeping) or losing your soul, or life. He challenges us with a paradox: if you want to have life, let it go. If you hold on to it, you will lose it. Jim Elliot, the late missionary to the Auca Indians, penned a well-known paraphrase to this paradox: "He is no fool who gives what he cannot keep to gain that which he cannot lose."[3] By using a paradox, Jesus drives us toward a decision. The answer to the paradox continues the theme of verse 34, namely: do we hold on to our life in our own self-centered way or do we release the tight grip on our self-determination and instead trust the one who created us?

Mark 8:36–37 develops this theme further. Jesus questions whether we can keep our soul alive in God by gaining the whole world. Whatever we might gain in our lives, it is nothing compared with forfeiting our soul. What good is it for us to gain whatever we would pursue and lose that which God offers us in the form of true, enduring life? Forfeiting our life, then, is living in a God-alien, self-sufficient way that contradicts the fundamental basis of our lives, namely, to walk in dependence on God for his glory.

A deeper exploration of Mark 8:34–37 leads to the conclusion that a thorough surrender of the central control over ourselves means not only to see and seek Christ's person and ways (see the discussion of Bonhoeffer below). It includes the recognition that Jesus values us so much that he entrusts us with the awesome responsibility of taking care of ourselves as stewards, parallel to loving our neighbor (Lev. 19:18). This is clearly suggested in Mark 8:35–37, which emphasizes the irredeemable and irreducible value of human life and the opportunity of truly gaining life.

Furthermore, the value of human life is most fundamentally emphasized by the fact that God values us so much as to give the life of Jesus, his eternal Son, for ours. At the heart of this issue lies the following question: Why would Jesus die for us if we were

---

3. Elisabeth Elliot, *In the Shadow of the Almighty* (London: Hodder & Stoughton, 1958), 108.

not valuable in his eyes? Why would Jesus pursue us in relentless love if we were not valuable to him (see Matt. 6:26; 10:31; 12:12; Luke 12:7, 24)? The profound problem concerning human existence is not solved by Jesus declaring us valueless or by calling us into nothingness. Rather, Jesus restores us to value in the call to surrender self-sufficient enmity against God and find life in dependence upon him. God loves his creation dearly. John states: "For God so loved the world, that he gave his only begotten Son, that whoever believes in him should not perish but have eternal life" (John 3:16). Jesus suffers and dies for his creation. Nothing is held back to bring his creation back to himself. Paul says (Rom. 8:32): "He who did not spare his own Son but gave him up for us all, how will he not also with him graciously give us all things?"

"Denying yourself" in this context of divine affirmation means the severing of old ties and letting go of idols (again, see the material on Bonhoeffer below) because we have been loved so profoundly by Christ. It means that we surrender to be fully embraced by a dying and resurrected shepherd and co-creator.

Jesus spoke metaphorically of the seed (self) that must die in order to bear fruit: "Truly, truly, I say to you, unless a grain of wheat falls into the earth and dies, it remains alone; but if it dies, it bears much fruit" (John 12:24). It is true that the outer shell of the seed must break open, but the seed is not so much annihilated as it is utterly given over to bearing fruit. God uses his inspired Word, his Spirit, the sacraments, other people, and circumstances to bring our self-determination to such death. The surrender of this central control then leads to community and to addressing social justice issues which conform to God's kingdom mission. The hermeneutical key to the cost of discipleship is thus not self-deprecation but surrender of self-determination.

As Bonhoeffer rightly states, our focus does indeed need to be on Christ. In full surrender of the central control over ourselves, in full and ongoing dependence upon the triune God who has come close in Christ, we are, however, to take good care of others and of ourselves as gifts from God. In ongoing dependence on

184

Christ, not trusting in our own resources, we are to love others and ourselves, as Christ so deeply loves us.

Some may argue that to love ourselves as stewards of what belongs to Christ may come perilously close to narcissism and may imply a contradiction of Jesus' call to deny ourselves and to take up our cross. Indeed, we must guard against selfishness and narcissism. However, Jesus points sufficiently to the disciples' self-sufficiency as well as their value in his eyes to warrant our dual emphasis.

As we focus on Christ, we must keep ourselves, as God-dependent stewards, in peripheral vision, guarding our hearts, thus learning to treat ourselves as God-loved creatures (John 3:16).

In Jesus' call to discipleship he names the root problem standing in the way of that reversal of alienation. Getting at the root problem is not to reject ourselves, or to abase ourselves. Rather, we are to reject our persistent self-reliance and our pernicious autonomy. We are called to hand over the keys of our prodigal self-determination, which Adam, Eve, and you and I have willfully forced from the fatherly hand of God in the first place. We are called to return to the mode of living that our Creator intended in ongoing God-dependence.

In this way the essential dilemma of human existence is squarely addressed: Jesus takes the poisonous, autonomous control away from us and, surprisingly, re-entrusts us, in ongoing dependence upon him, as stewards who continuously carry their crosses of an ended life and learn to reflect him in a new life.

Paying the cost of discipleship leads most profoundly to affirming the goodness of creation gone wrong. Christ did not come to deny the value of each person on this globe; he came to remove their ugly enmity and willful resistance. To pay the cost of discipleship is a necessary consequence of his sacrificial death for us: first he dies an atoning, substitutionary death and then he bids us surrender all that stands in the way of his ongoing love for us.

The chief enemy that needs to be radically denied and crucified is thus not our value as creatures in God's eyes, but our illegitimate, God-defying control over ourselves. This chief enemy can be seen in humankind's history, the history of philosophy, psychological models, ideologies, and naturalistic worldviews of some proponents of modern science.

Bernard of Clairvaux, in *On Loving God*, says: first, man loves himself for his own sake; then, man loves God for self's sake; then, man loves God for God's sake; and finally, man loves himself solely for God's sake.[4]

As followers of Christ, we will never again take ourselves back as our own possession. Paul says of Jesus that he "gave himself for us to redeem us from all lawlessness and to purify for himself a people for his own possession who are zealous for good works" (Titus 2:14). Peter states: "But you are . . . a people for his own possession, that you may proclaim the excellencies of him who called you out of darkness into his marvelous light" (1 Peter 2:9). We are not permitted to "repossess" ourselves. Much of our suffering is the attempt, in the face of God's freeing mercy, to seek to repossess ourselves against his kingdom will.

Jesus' sacrifice places profound and lasting value on human life. It also calls that life to its original design: from ugly alienation to loving reconciliation; from harsh autonomy to reconciled dependence; from bitter enmity against God, self, and others to life-giving shalom. God's embrace of us in Christ's atoning death means love overcoming self-defensive, self-preserving resistance. As such, we will indeed suffer much external opposition, ridicule, persecution, and, yes, even physical death. Rather than to abandon ourselves, Christ calls us in denying ourselves and in carrying our cross to fully surrender to his matchless and enduring love.

Reflections on Dietrich Bonhoeffer's *The Cost of Discipleship*[5]

Given the facts of Dietrich Bonhoeffer's life, it is appropriate to ask who might have the moral stature to comment on aspects of his

4. See Bernard of Clairvaux (1090–1153), *On Loving God*, chapter xv (early 12th century).

5. In the following assessment of Bonhoeffer, I do not discuss his entire theology, the question of what exact theological position he held during his early and later years,

important and influential book *The Cost of Discipleship* and on the views expressed in it, some of which coincide with and some of which contrast with our own.[6] Who can come close to a man who had the opportunity to remain at a safe distance from Nazi Germany, with its dictatorial and utterly ruthless destruction of 6 million Jews and 44 additional millions of people from various other lands, and yet who thrust himself into the center of that horrific milieu? In 1939, Bonhoeffer could have remained safely in New York, writing and teaching fruitfully. Instead, he took the last scheduled steamship before the start of World War II back to the heart of German evil. There he eventually faced the ethical dilemma of collaborating in one of the last assassination attempts on Adolf Hitler on July 20, 1944.

Bonhoeffer's life is so compelling that one hardly dare ask searching questions concerning his stance on the "cost of discipleship." After all, Bonhoeffer paid that cost, not only when he was hanged at the Flossenburg concentration camp on April 9, 1945, just a few weeks before German surrender, but long before that point. In fact, many choices in his all too brief life of 39 years are marked by sacrifice and far-reaching surrender. Here are but a few examples:

- He decided to enter the pastoral ministry despite critical comments from his well-situated, greatly respected family.[7]
- He returned to Nazi Germany from London in 1935.
- He returned from New York to Germany in 1939 at the onset of the carnage that Hitler and his co-criminals set in motion.
- Bonhoeffer did not only write on the cost of discipleship; above all, he lived it, not least at the Finkenwalde underground seminary while defying Nazi pressure. Especially from 1935 to 1937 and then as a "fugitive professor" from 1937 to 1939, he instructed many German

and particularly the complex question of what his theological views were a few months before he was hanged.

6. The most recent edition of this book is simply entitled *Discipleship* (Minneapolis: Fortress Press, 2003). Our references pertain to Dietrich Bonhoeffer, *The Cost of Discipleship* (New York: Macmillan, 1966).

7. His father was a distinguished neurologist and professor in Berlin.

seminarians and encouraged them in their respective callings. During the Finkenwalde time, he repeatedly asked
his students whether it was ethically justifiable, under any
circumstance, to seek to kill one man if it meant averting
great evil and untold destruction.

By the time he began to ask these questions, Bonhoeffer was
already deeply involved with a ring of German Military Intelligence
officers who were secretly working in the German resistance against
the SS and Hitler. To the very end he implied, self-critically, that his
involvement in the German resistance, particularly his involvement
in the assassination attempt on Hitler, was tainted with moral guilt.

Bonhoeffer's influence was and remains profound. As an
example, we quote here one of Bonhoeffer's candid statements:

> If our Christianity has ceased to be serious about discipleship,
> if we have watered down the gospel into emotional uplift which
> makes no costly demands and which fails to distinguish between
> natural and Christian existence, then we cannot help regarding
> the cross as an ordinary everyday calamity, as one of the trials
> and tribulations of life.[8]

Precisely because I greatly admire Bonhoeffer's views on
the cost of discipleship, I will submit two suggestions which I
deem fitting complements, or perhaps modifications, to his views.
These suggestions will be based on what we have stated above
concerning "denying yourself" and "carrying your cross" (Mark
8:34) and will, I trust, affirm much of what he lived and wrote
on the cost of discipleship.

Affirmations and Questions

The call to—and cost of—discipleship is, as Bonhoeffer
states, radical and fundamental. To be ready for Christ and his
ways requires a repeated severing of old ties, which include finding

8. Bonhoeffer, *Cost of Discipleship*, 88–89.

safety in possessions, desires, power, and fame. It also includes the willingness to suffer and, if necessary, to die.[9]

Bonhoeffer rightly states: "The first Christ-suffering which every man must experience is the call to abandon the attachments of the world."[10] We must thus die to our selfish affections and lusts.[11] "The yoke and the burden of Christ are his cross."[12] "To go one's way under the sign of the cross is not misery and desperation, but peace and refreshment for the soul. It is the highest joy. Then we do not walk under our self-made laws and burdens, but under the yoke of him who knows us and who walks under the yoke with us. Under his yoke we are certain of his nearness and communion."[13] "We can of course shake off the burden which is laid upon us, but only find that we have a still heavier burden to carry—a yoke of our own choosing, the yoke of self."[14] Elsewhere he states pointedly: "Denying yourself is not just a series of isolated acts of mortification or asceticism: for there is an element of self-will even in that."[15]

Yet, while agreeing with Bonhoeffer concerning the radical nature of severing ties and paying the cost of discipleship, we must ask the following question: What precisely is Christ asking us to sacrifice?

I am convinced that Jesus calls us not only to surrender our old ways of finding safety (in possessions, desires, and reputation) and to be ready to suffer and die. Jesus, essentially, calls for the surrender of a self-generated, self-determined life and the willingness to accept wherever that deep surrender leads. He calls us to surrender the central control (mind and heart) over ourselves.[16] If we see the cost of discipleship essentially from this vantage point, all the aspects Bonhoeffer mentions are true, and perhaps a bit more clearly focused.

---

9. In the Christian faith there is, however, no ethical room for a definition of martyrdom that justifies random suicide bombings of innocent people such as is common in some religious factions.

10. Bonhoeffer, *Cost of Discipleship*, 89.

11. Ibid., 90.

12. Ibid., 93.

13. Ibid.

14. Ibid., 92–93.

15. Ibid., 88.

16. Bonhoeffer comes closest to this when he alludes to the surrender of self-will.

Suggestions regarding the Meaning of "Carrying Your Cross" and "Denying Yourself"

Certainly, following Christ includes our willingness to suffer, to bear shame, and to experience persecution.[17] Bonhoeffer says: "The cross means sharing the suffering of Christ to the last and to the fullest."[18] "Suffering [is a] . . . badge of true discipleship"; it means to "lose our lives in his service."[19] But, as demonstrated above, "carrying your cross" is more essentially a call to surrender control of self. It means, fundamentally, living a life which Christ possesses.

A second aspect of Bonhoeffer's description of the cost of discipleship is quite sensitive and merits careful exploration. It centers on his explanation of the meaning of "denying yourself." Bonhoeffer states: "To deny oneself is to be aware only of Christ and no more of self, to see only him who goes before and no more the road which is too hard for us. Once more, all that self-denial can say is: 'He leads the way, keep close to him.'" Elsewhere he states: "Only when we have become completely oblivious of self are we ready to bear the cross for his sake. If in the end we know only him, if we have ceased to notice the pain of our own cross, we are indeed looking only unto him."[20]

Regarding this second issue, I find cause to differ more directly with Bonhoeffer. Knowing how strongly he embraced the goodness of God's beautiful creation and the goodness of life,[21] however, I do wonder whether Bonhoeffer would agree with our reflections on Mark 8:34–37, in which we argued that, contrary to self-deprecation, paying the cost of discipleship includes taking loving care of ourselves and others as those loved by God in the context of radical surrender to his will.

Mark 8:34 (together with vv. 35–37) helps us to see clearly both the radical nature of what it means to follow Christ and the great value of human life.

17. Bonhoeffer, *Cost of Discipleship*, 87.
18. Ibid., 89.
19. Ibid., 91.
20. Ibid., 88.
21. See, e.g., Bonhoeffer, *Life Together* (London: SCM Press, 1949), 19–20.

Questions for Study
and Reflection[1]

QUESTIONS AND COMMENTS in regular type are meant to facilitate further understanding; questions and comments in italics are primarily meant for personal and communal application and appropriation. Note: There are no questions for the Introduction.

Chapter 1—Mark as Biography and Memorized Witness Account

1. What is the purpose of studing Mark's literary features?

2. Describe the significance of Mark as an ancient biography (*bios*).

3. Why is it significant that Jesus sought to embed his teaching (by action and word) in the memory of his original disciples?

Chapter 2—Mark's Structure, Purpose, and Flow of Thought

1. What significance lies in the fact that Mark is a narrative?

2. What are significant factors of Mark's outline and structure?

3. Describe Mark's plot development.

4. What is Mark's chief purpose?

5. Give a brief description of Mark's flow of thought.

---

1. Some of these questions were developed in collaboration with Donald Guthrie, Susan Bayer, and Mark Stirling. I acknowledge their contribution with great gratitude.

Chapter 3—Mark's Thematic Framework: The In-Breaking of God's Eternal Rule

1. Why is it important to understand different expectations of the kingdom of God at the time of Jesus?

2. Describe the most prevalent expectation of the kingdom of God at the time of Jesus.

3. Give some characteristics of Jesus' teaching on the kingdom of God.

4. Why is it helpful to speak about the rule of God?

Chapter 4—Witness to the Unique Person of Jesus

1. Characterize the primary and most popular expectation of the Messiah at the time of Jesus.

2. How is Jesus as "Son of God" characterized in Mark?

3. How is Jesus as "Son of Man" characterized in Mark?

4. Why does the Son of Man *have* to die?

5. Where does the origin of "Jesus as Lord" lie according to Mark?

6. Describe the relationship between Jesus' teaching on the kingdom of God and the Messiah of God.

7. *What is the significance of studying the person of Christ for discipleship?*

Chapter 5—Jesus' Fundamental Challenge to the Twelve and to All Disciples

1. Describe the double crisis of self-perception and God-perception in terms of Jesus' teaching of the disciples *and in personal terms.*

2. What is the figurative meaning of "yeast"? What does that say about *you*?

3. What is the figurative meaning of "seeing" and "hearing"? What does that say about *you*?

4. What are the popular views of Christ (Mark 8:27–28)? Explain.

5. How does Peter's confession (Mark 8:29) differ from the popular views?

6. Contrast the "radiance of Moses" (Exod. 34:29–35) with that of Jesus in the transfiguration account (Mark 9:2–8).

7. Why is Jesus leading *you/us* into a double crisis? How does he resolve it?

8. Describe the communal effect of the resolution of the double crisis. How does this challenge *you*?

9. Describe the ongoing nature of discipleship (see also chapter 6). How does this affect *you*?

Chapter 6—Christlike Character

1. Describe the reasons for the claim that the core character traits apply to *all* disciples.

2. How does Jesus teach, exemplify, and engender core character traits in his original disciples and in contemporary followers?

3. List the eight core character traits found in Mark and give a brief description of each.

Chapter 7—Eight Discipleship Qualities

1. Describe what it means to *you* personally to surrender and follow God's will in response to his love:

    a. To what extent are *you* surrendered/surrendering to God? To what extent are you obedient before God?

    b. What attitudes or issues might hinder *you* from surrendering to Jesus?

    c. How do *you* feel about handing over ownership of every part of your life to him?

    d. To what extent does this affect *your* relationship with others and yourself?

2. What is the goal of Mark 8:34?

    a. What is the meaning of "carrying your cross"? *Explain personally.* See also Matthew 11:28–30.

    b. What is the meaning of "denying yourself"? *Explain personally.*

3. What does it mean to *you* to "lose one's life"?

4. What is the connection between Jesus' call to follow and his person and work?

5. How does Jesus' resolution of the double crisis relate to the core character trait of surrender?

6. Describe what it means to believe and trust in God.

7. What attitudes or issues might hinder a person from trusting and believing Jesus?

8. In light of Christ's love:

    a. How do *you* personally react to the call to trust and believe?

    b. In which concrete areas of life do *you* hesitate in trusting in God?

    c. How might *you* help or encourage others to trust and believe to Jesus?

9. In view of who calls us to trust and believe, how might *your* community be affected as individuals trust and believe in Jesus?

10. Describe in *personal* terms what it means to be prayerful.

11. In light of Christ's love:

    a. To what extent are *you* praying to God?
    b. To what extent does *your* prayer life remain a reality as you relate to others and yourself?

12. What would a list of reversals of the heart-defilements described in Mark 7:20–23 look like?

13. Describe in *personal* terms what it means to watch over your heart (see 1 Tim. 4:15–16).

14. What heart-defilements (Mark 7:20–23) do *you* personally struggle with?

15. In response to Jesus' love:

    a. To what extent do *you* maintain watchfulness over your heart before God as you relate to others and yourself?
    b. To what extent are *you* able to help others learn to watch their own hearts?

16. Describe in *personal* terms what it means to serve humbly.

17. In response to Jesus' love:

    a. To what extent are *you* humbly serving God?
    b. To what extent do *you* exemplify this to others?

18. Describe in *personal* terms what it means to forgive.

19. What is the difference between forgiveness and reconciliation?

20. In light of Jesus' love:

    a. To what extend do *you* accept that you are forgiven by God?
    b. In what areas do *you* concretely need to forgive yourself and others? In what areas are you unable to forgive? Why?
    c. How can *you* convey forgiveness to others and help them also to live it out?

21. Describe in *personal* terms what it means to withstand temptation and to be watchful.

22. In light of Jesus' love:

    a. To what extent are *you* withstanding temptation and being watchful before God?
    b. To what extent does this remain a reality as *you* withstand temptation and remain watchful in human relationships?

23. Describe in *personal* terms what it means to confess Christ and to proclaim him courageously.

24. In light of Jesus' love, to what extent does confessing Christ remain a reality as *you* relate to other human beings?

Chapter 8—A Reciprocal Approach to Discipleship

1. Characterize and describe a "reciprocal approach" to discipleship.

2. List ways that you can *apply this to your life*.

Chapter 9—Following Mark's Call in the Twenty-first Century

1. Name the three basic categories of contemporary spirituality (especially in the Western world).

2. Relate these three basic categories to the following discipleship dynamics in Mark:

    a. The double crisis of self-perception and God-perception.
    b. Jesus' resolution of the double crisis.
    c. The eight core characteristics of discipleship-formation in Mark.

3. How would *you* explain the nature of discipleship to a representative of any of the named trends in contemporary spirituality?

Select Resources

Adsit, Christopher. *Personal Disciple-Making: A Step-by-Step Guide for Leading a Christian from New Birth to Maturity*. Nashville: Thomas Nelson, 1988.

Ali, Ayaan Hirsi. *Infidel*. New York: Free Press, 2007.

Arn, Win, and Charles Arn. *The Master's Plan for Making Disciples: Every Christian an Effective Witness Through an Enabling Church*. 2nd. ed. Grand Rapids: Baker, 1998.

Augsburger, David W. *Dissident Discipleship: A Spirituality of Self-Surrender, Love of God, and Love of Neighbor*. Grand Rapids: Brazos Books, 2006.

Baxter, Richard. *The Reformed Pastor*. Carlisle, PA: Banner of Truth Trust, 1974.

Benner, David. *The Gift of Being Yourself: The Sacred Call to Self-Discovery*. Downers Grove, IL: InterVarsity Press, 2004.

Bly, Stephen A. *Radical Discipleship: Tough Standards for Spiritual Greatness*. Chicago: Moody Press, 1981.

Boice, James M. *Christ's Call to Discipleship*. Minneapolis: Grason, 1986.

Bonhoeffer, Dietrich. *The Cost of Discipleship*. New York: Macmillan, 1966. (Now published as *Dietrich Bonhoeffer Works*, Vol. 4: *Discipleship*. Edited by Geffrey B. Kelly and John D. Godsey. Minneapolis: Fortress, 2003.)

Bridges, Jerry. *The Practice of Godliness*. Colorado Springs: NavPress, 1985.

_____. *The Pursuit of Holiness*. Colorado Springs: NavPress, 1978.

Briscoe, Stuart. *Everyday Discipleship for Ordinary People*. Wheaton, IL: Harold Shaw, 1988.

Bruce, Alexander B. *The Training of the Twelve*. Grand Rapids: Kregel, 2000 [1894].

Brueggemann, Walter. *The Word That Redescribes the World: The Bible and Discipleship*. Edited by Patrick D. Miller. Minneapolis: Augsburg Fortress, 2006.

Calhoun, Adele Ahlberg. *Spiritual Disciplines Handbook: Practices That Transform Us*. Downers Grove, IL: InterVarsity Press, 2005.

Chantry, Walter J. *The Shadow of the Cross: Studies in Self-Denial*. Carlisle, PA: Banner of Truth, 1981.

Coleman, Robert E. *The Master Plan of Evangelism*. Grand Rapids: Revell, 2010 (orig. Grand Rapids: Baker, 1963).

Coppedge, Allan. *The Biblical Principles of Discipleship*. Grand Rapids: Francis Asbury Press, 1989.

Delsol, Chantal. *Icarus Fallen: The Search For Meaning in an Uncertain World*. Translated by Robin Dick. 2nd ed. Wilmington, DE: Intercollegiate Studies Institute, 2010.

Eberstadt, Mary. "How the West Really Lost God," *Policy Review* 143 (July 1, 2007): 3–20.

Eims, LeRoy. *The Lost Art of Disciple Making*. Colorado Springs: NavPress, 1978.

Forman, Rowland, Jeff Jones, and Bruce Miller. *The Leadership Baton: An Intentional Strategy for Developing Leaders in Your Church*. Grand Rapids: Zondervan, 2004.

Foss, Michael W. *Power Surge: Six Marks of Discipleship for a Changing Church*. Minneapolis: Fortress, 2000.

Foster, Richard J. *Celebration of Discipline: The Path to Spiritual Growth*. San Francisco: HarperSanFrancisco, 1998 [1978].

Fryling, Alice, ed. *Disciplemakers' Handbook: Helping People Grow in Christ*. Downers Grove, IL: InterVarsity Press, 1989.

Gorman, Michael J. *Cruciformity: Paul's Narrative Spirituality of the Cross*. Grand Rapids: Eerdmans, 2001.

Guyon, Jeanne. *Experiencing the Depths of Jesus Christ*. Goleta, CA: Christian Books, 1981 [1685].

Habermas, Ronald T. *The Complete Disciple: A Model for Cultivating God's Image in Us*. London: Chariot Victor, 2003.

Hendrichsen, Walter A. *Disciples Are Made Not Born*. Colorado Springs: Cook Communications, 1974.

Hull, Bill. *Choose the Life: Exploring a Faith That Embraces Discipleship*. Grand Rapids: Baker, 2004.

_____. *The Complete Book of Discipleship: On Being and Making Followers of Christ*. Colorado Springs: NavPress, 2006.

_____. *The Disciple-Making Church*. Grand Rapids: Fleming Revell, 1990.

_____. *The Disciple-Making Pastor*. Grand Rapids: Revell, 1999 [1988].

_____. *Jesus Christ, Disciplemaker*. Grand Rapids: Baker, 2004.

Jenkins, Peter. *The Next Christendom: The Coming of Global Christianity*. Oxford: Oxford University Press, 2002.

Krallmann, Günter. *Mentoring for Mission: A Handbook on Leadership Principles Exemplified by Jesus Christ*. Waynesboro, GA: Authentic Media, 2002.

Kuhne, Gary W. *The Dynamics of Discipleship Training: Being and Producing Spiritual Leaders*. Grand Rapids: Zondervan, 1978.

Longenecker, Richard. *Patterns of Discipleship in the New Testament*. Grand Rapids: Eerdmans, 1996.

Macaulay, Ranald, and Jerram Barrs. *Being Human: The Nature of Spiritual Experience*. Downers Grove, IL: InterVarsity Press, 1978.

McGrath, Alister. *A Passion for Truth: The Intellectual Coherence of Evangelicalism*. Downers Grove, IL: InterVarsity Press, 1996.

Moore, Waylon B. *Multiplying Disciples: The New Testament Method of Church Growth*. Tampa, FL: Missions Unlimited, 1981.

Newbigin, Lesslie. *Proper Confidence: Faith, Doubt, and Certainty in Christian Discipleship*. Grand Rapids: Eerdmans, 1995.

Noll, Mark A. *The Scandal of the Evangelical Mind*. Grand Rapids: Eerdmans, 1994.

Nouwen, Henry. *Reaching Out: The Three Movements of the Spiritual Life*. New York: Doubleday, 1975.

Ogden, Greg. *Discipleship Essentials: A Guide to Building Your Life in Christ*. Downers Grove, IL: InterVarsity Press, 1998.

_____. *Transforming Discipleship: Making Disciples a Few at a Time*. Downers Grove, IL: InterVarsity Press, 2003.

Ortberg, John. *The Life You've Always Wanted: Spiritual Disciplines for Ordinary People*. Grand Rapids: Zondervan, 2002.

Packer, James I. *Knowing God*. Downers Grove, IL: InterVarsity Press, 1975.

Pagels, Elaine. *The Gnostic Gospels*. New York: Vintage Books, 1979.

Petersen, Jim. *Lifestyle Discipleship: The Challenge of Following Jesus in Today's World*. Colorado Springs: NavPress, 2007 [1993].

Peterson, Eugene H. *Practice Resurrection: A Conversation on Growing Up in Christ*. Grand Rapids: Eerdmans, 2010.

Robinson, Martin, and Dwight Smith. *Invading Secular Space: Strategies for Tomorrow's Church*. Grand Rapids: Monarch Books, 2003.

Royal, Robert. *The God That Did Not Fail: How Religion Built and Sustains the West*. New York: Encounter Books, 2006.

Sanders, J. Oswalt. *Spiritual Discipleship: Principles of Following Christ for Every Believer*. Chicago: Moody Bible Institute, 1990.

Schaeffer, Francis. *True Spirituality*. Wheaton, IL: Tyndale House, 1971.

Smallman, Stephen. *The Walk: Steps for New and Renewed Followers of Jesus*. Phillipsburg, NJ: P&R Publishing, 2009.

Stanley, Paul D., and J. Robert Clinton. *Connecting: The Mentoring Relationships You Need to Succeed in Life*. Colorado Springs: NavPress, 1992.

Tozer, A. W. *The Pursuit of God*. Harrisburg, PA: Christian Publication, 1948.

Tripp, Paul D. *Instruments in the Redeemer's Hands*. Phillipsburg, NJ: P&R Publishing, 2002.

Trueblood, Elton. *The Incendiary Fellowship*. San Francisco: Harper-SanFrancisco, 1978.

Watson, David. *Covenant Discipleship: Christian Formation through Mutual Accountability*. Eugene, OR: Wipf & Stock Publishers, 2002.

Weigel, George. "Europe's Problem and Ours," *First Things* (Feb. 2004): 21–25.

Whitney, Donald. *Spiritual Disciplines for the Christian Life*. Colorado Springs: NavPress, 1991.

Wilhoit, James C. *Spiritual Formation as if the Church Mattered: Growing in Christ through Community*. Grand Rapids: Baker, 2008.

Wilkins, Michael J. *Following the Master: A Biblical Theology of Discipleship*. Grand Rapids: Zondervan, 1992.

Willard, Dallas. *The Divine Conspiracy: Rediscovering Our Hidden Life in God*. San Francisco: HarperSanFrancisco, 1998.

_____. *The Great Omission: Reclaiming Jesus' Essential Teachings on Discipleship*. San Francisco: HarperSanFrancisco, 2006.

_____. *Renovation of the Heart: Putting on the Character of Christ*. Colorado Springs: NavPress, 2002.

_____. *The Spirit of the Disciples*. San Francisco: HarperOne, 1991.

Wright, Christopher J. H. *The Mission of God: Unlocking the Bible's Grand Narrative*. Downers Grove, IL: InterVarsity Press, 2006.

Yoder, John Howard. *Discipleship as Political Responsibility*. Scottdale, PA: Herald Press, 2003.

Index of Scripture

Ephesians
1:5—50n10
2:11–21—129
4:1–16—84
4:11–16—126, 132

Philippians
1:9–11—112
2:1–4—182
2:1–5—126, 130
2:5–7—49
2:5–8—120
2:5–11—51
2:8–11—55
3:9–10—182
4:8—111

Colossians
1:21–22—76, 114
2:11–14—86
2:23—67n13
3:1—86
3:1–17—157, 182
3:5—86, 127
3:10—76, 86
4:7ff—173
4:10—169, 173, 175,
    180n69
4:14—180n69

1 Thessalonians
1:1—174

2 Thessalonians
1:1—174

1 Timothy
1:15—86
4:7—112
4:16—112

2 Timothy
4:11—173n51, 174, 175,
    180n69
4:11–12—173

Titus
2:14—186

Philemon
23–24—175
24—173, 180n69

Hebrews
4:14–15—50
4:14–16—86
5:7—94n7
5:7–9—50
7:5—96, 110
11:25—86
12:1—86
12:4—86
13:8—91

James
1:15—86
5:14–16—86

1 Peter
1:3—151
2:9—186
2:24—86
3:15—121
5:12—174
5:12–13—174n52
5:13—170, 173, 173n51, 174,
    175

2 Peter
1:16–17—50n9
1:16–18—49

Index of Subjects and Names